Guidelines for Excellence® in Management
The Manager's Digest

Edited by
John M. Ivancevich
William Lidwell

THOMSON
TEXERE

Australia · Canada · Mexico · Singapore · Spain · United Kingdom · United States

Guidelines for Excellence® in Management: The Manager's Digest

John M. Ivancevich and William Lidwell, editors

COPYRIGHT © 2004 by Texere, an imprint of Thomson Higher Education, a part of The Thomson Corporation.

Published in 2004 by TEXERE, part of the Thomson Corporation. TEXERE, Thomson, and Thomson logo, are trademarks used herein under license.

ISBN: 0-324-27149-2
Printed and bound in the United States by Phoenix Book Technology
1 2 3 4 5 7 8 9 07 06 05 04

For more information, contact Texere, 622 Third Avenue, 10th Floor, New York, NY 10017, or find us on the Web at www.etexere.com.

Composed by: ATLIS Graphics
Library of Congress Cataloging in Publication Data: Has been applied for.

BRIEF CONTENTS

CONTENTS

FOREWORD

The primary goal of this book is to provide readers with clear and unqualified guidance regarding how best to practice management. This guidance is presented in the form of guidelines, which represent a distillation of much of what is currently known both practically and empirically about management. Managers who follow these guidelines will, on average, be more effective than managers who do not. Organizations that follow these guidelines will, on average, outperform organizations that do not.

This book is divided into three sections: direction, execution, and people. This simple organization is intended to help managers focus on those aspects of management that are most critical to success. The direction section contains guidelines regarding strategy, leadership, and governance. The execution section contains guidelines regarding process, structure, and teams. The people section contains guidelines regarding employee acquisition, retention, development, and productivity. The guidelines are indexed within each of these sections for convenient reference.

The guidelines in this book are not like laws of physics or principles of mathematics that are true in all cases all of the time. Nor are the guidelines like "best practices" that have been observed to be true for one organization and may or may not be true for other organizations. Guidelines are true in most cases most of the time. There will be exceptions—i.e., circumstances in which a particular guideline should not be applied. The reader must ultimately determine when to apply and when to disregard a guideline. However, we encourage the practice of being able to explain to peers the reasons behind a decision to disregard. To disregard a guideline with good reason is excellent management. To disregard a guideline with poor or no reason is malpractice.

Many practicing managers today have no formal training in management. These managers should take heart. They are not as disadvantaged as they may believe. Professionally trained managers generally perform no better than their untrained counterparts. With over 100 years of management-related research and experience, the state of the art in management today is perceived by most practitioners to lie somewhere between the leadership principles of some dead general and the coaching techniques that won last year's Super Bowl. The fact is that most practitioners are simply winging it—managing as they are managed or have been managed in the past.

What of the MBA? The unprecedented abundance of MBAs in the workplace has done little to ebb market bubbles, business failures, or corporate scandals. Research comparing the real-world performance of MBAs with non-MBAs in the workplace has found little difference. An MBA degree clearly provides value in terms of business literacy, job opportunities, and a network of contacts. Beyond these benefits, an MBA appears to offer little in terms of enabling managers to successfully build or manage organizations better than their non-MBA peers. This is less an indictment of MBA programs, however, than a symptom of an immature body of knowledge. Management is still very much art and very little science.

The secondary goal of this book is to begin the hard work of inverting this relationship. A first step toward this end is complete: many of the guidelines in this book double as clear, testable claims that can be corroborated or falsified. They do not represent all that is known about management. They do, however, represent a good bit of what is known. Some are likely not completely correct or complete. However, most of them are almost certainly correct and complete.

The trick, of course, is knowing which ones are which. And unfortunately, there is no "trick" to attain this knowledge. It will come only with time and the hard work of focused research. Thus, we invite members of the academic, research, and practitioner communities to engage this research. Through this process and the passage of time, a true science of management will emerge.

John M. Ivancevich

William Lidwell

CONTRIBUTORS

Marie-Hélène Budworth	University of Toronto
Warner Burke	Columbia University
Archie Carroll	University of Georgia
Myron Deily	Applied Management Sciences Institute
Tom Diamante	Adelphi University
Thomas Duening	University of Houston—Downtown
Robert Eichinger	Lominger Limited, Inc.
Gary Ely	Avista Corporation
Marsha Johnson Evans	American Red Cross
Sydney Finkelstein	Dartmouth College
Jacqueline Gilbert	Middle Tennessee State University
Richard Hackman	Harvard University
Brian Janz	University of Memphis
Robert Konopaske	The University of North Carolina—Wilmington
Gary Latham	University of Toronto
Edwin Locke	University of Maryland
Michael Lombardo	Center for Creative Leadership
Lee Preston	University of Maryland
Karlene Roberts	University of California at Berkeley
John Slocum	Southern Methodist University
Dean Tjosvold	Lingnan University
M. Cass Wheeler	American Heart Association
Dave Ulrich	University of Michigan
James Wetherbe	Texas Tech University

USE

MANAGERS

The guidelines in this book can help managers and their organizations improve performance. Comparing the guidelines with organizational practice provide valuable opportunities for understanding and improving the organization. Here are a few suggestions on how this book can be used by managers:

- *Train managers and employees*
  Educate managers and employees about the guidelines. Organizations perform at their best when everyone is using the same playbook.
- *Evaluate organizational practices*
  Assign individuals or groups to compare organizational practices with guidelines. When they conflict, ask the individuals or groups to identify the reasons why the conflict is justified or to modify the practice.
- *Support decisions*
  Cite guidelines to support decisions and initiatives within the organization—especially when the decisions are difficult or unpopular.
- *Review and self-evaluate*
  Review guidelines to gain insight into different ways of approaching management problems. Use these insights for self-evaluation and self-coaching.
- *Adopt guidelines for excellence as an organization*
  Consider adopting the guidelines in this book as an organization. Adapt guidelines to better fit the needs of the organization. Hold managers and staff accountable for implementing and observing them.

These suggestions are intended to directly impact the performance of managers and their organizations. The outcome should be measurable improvements in standard measures of performance, including productivity, retention, growth, and profitability.

USE

EDUCATORS

The guidelines in this book can help students learn about the effective practice of management. Practicing and critiquing the guidelines in a classroom setting coupled with observing and testing them in real contexts provide a valuable learning experience. Here are a few suggestions on how this book can be used by educators:

- *Examine theory and research*
  Assign individuals or groups to examine the evidence behind different guidelines and to report their findings.
- *Corroborate or falsify guidelines*
  As individuals or teams, present evidence and argue the case for or against selected guidelines.
- *Role-play*
  Develop role-play scenarios in which students apply and act out guidelines. The class can critique the role play and discuss the abilities and skills that participants should strengthen.
- *Interview managers*
  Assign students to interview practitioners about a specific guideline or set of guidelines. Does the manager use the guidelines or something similar? How? Why? When? Have the students prepare and present a report on their findings to the class.
- *Develop additional guidelines*
  Establish teams to work on the development of additional guidelines using the same architecture and standards used in this book. The group's additions can be rated and graded on the following criteria: strength of evidence, relevance, practicality, and ethics/legality.

These suggestions are intended to improve learning through in-class or out-of-class exercises and interactions. The outcome should be the expansion of knowledge about guidelines, as well as evaluative skills that govern their use.

ACKNOWLEDGMENTS

This book is a collective work. It is the product of numerous contributors who worked hard to present managers with a simple, usable set of guidelines to improve the practice of management. It is the product of numerous reviewers who worked hard to ensure that the guidelines were relevant, practical, and readable. Finally, it is the product of the publishing and editorial support provided by the people at South-Western Publishing and the Applied Management Sciences Institute. To synthesize the many inputs provided by these groups has been the job of the editors. After reviewing all of the guidelines and reviewer feedback, we made the final decisions about which guidelines were included and excluded. Additionally, we edited the submissions in order to present readers with guidelines that are consistent in both style and substance. Any errors of omission or commission in this process are ours and ours alone. We hope this book meets with the approval of all of these participants. Without their hard work and dedication, it would not have been possible.

John M. Ivancevich

William Lidwell

1.0 DIRECTION

What employees want most from their leaders are direction and meaning, trust, and hope. Every good leader I have spoken with had a willful determination to achieve a set of goals, a set of convictions about what he or she wanted his or her organization to achieve. Everyone had a purpose. —*Warren Bennis*

This section presents guidelines to help organizations achieve coherent direction through sound governance, strategy, and leadership. The plans, activities, and interactions that arise from coherent direction enable organizations to develop a core competency, realize operational synergies through consolidation and focus, and ultimately achieve market leadership.

Take, for example, Medtronic, Inc. Medtronic was founded in 1949. It began as a medical equipment repair company located in a 600-square-foot garage in Minneapolis, Minnesota. It later began to sell equipment, and by the 1960s, it became a manufacturer of medical devices. Medtronic realized impressive growth throughout the seventies, eighties, and nineties using a combination of aggressive research and development and company acquisitions to establish leadership positions in target markets. By the end of the nineties, Medtronic had revenues of over $5 billion and a market capitalization in excess of $60 billion.

In 1999, Medtronic initiated a project to define a new direction for the company. It was called Medtronic Vision 2010. Vision 2010 began by involving employee representatives from all levels and all parts of the organization. These employees were grouped into specific teams to examine various aspects of the business and to predict how the company might change by 2010. Each team was encouraged to reach outside the company and to incorporate new thinking. Steve Mahle, president of the Cardiac Rhythm Management unit of Medtronic, summarized the value of creating a focused direction this way:

> *. . . in mountain climbing, it is always helpful to be able to look up periodically and see the summit. But, seeing the summit is not enough. To get there I have to figure out how to get over this boulder or up this ledge. My willingness to do all this and*

not get discouraged is reinforced by my ability to look and say, "okay, I see the goal, I know where I'm going, and I'm going there."

Success for Vision 2010 required the development of a clearly articulated direction for Medtronic. It also required the commitment of Medtronic employees. The Medtronic executive committee communicated the organization's vision and direction as suggested by the Vision 2010 team. Every Medtronic employee had access to the full report. The report stated that the direction of Medtronic was to be overseen by the board of directors and carried out by the organization's 30,000 employees.

At the time of the creation of Vision 2010, the Medtronic board conducted its own self-analysis and was already succession-planning for then-CEO Bill George. The board includes 2 internal directors and 12 external directors. It uses five committees to perform its work: corporate governance and nominating, audit, compensation, finance, and technology and quality. Committees are chaired by outside directors, who can serve no longer than three successive years. In terms of board composition, meeting frequency, independence of directors, and oversight role, the Medtronic board exemplifies good governance.

Medtronic is not as well known as organizations like General Electric, Vanguard, and Wal-Mart. However, Medtronic's performance in terms of shareholder value is as good as or better than its more publicized counterparts. Medtronic is successful because it practices management in a way that maximizes its chances of success. It follows internal guidelines that correspond very closely with what is believed to be the "optimal practice" regarding directing an organization. It follows guidelines much like the guidelines in this section.

1.1.1 KNOW WHAT BUSINESS YOU ARE IN

The failure to understand a market in terms of basic customer needs is perhaps the most fundamental and common mistake of management.

This failure is generally the result of three kinds of errors:

1. Confusion about the basic purpose of an organization—i.e., identifying and understanding customer needs and then innovating solutions to address them versus selling whatever solution the organization happens to create.
2. Lack of understanding about the core competency of the organization and how this competency can be leveraged and extended into broader contexts.
3. Arrogance and denial resulting from past successes, leading to an irrational commitment to failed offerings and an unwillingness to pursue new market opportunities.

Managers who know what business they are in avoid these errors by defining the business of the organization in terms of customer needs and then continuously developing new ways to address those needs. Managers do not, by contrast, define their business in terms of a specific product or service. For example, the railroads lost their once-dominant position in the transportation industry because they did not understand that they were in the transportation business—they thought they were in the railroad business. As the automotive and airline industries emerged and rapidly grew around them, the railroads did not seek to invest, innovate, or otherwise participate in these industries. Past success fostered a sense of invulnerability and denial. They continued their focus on laying rail and building trains. However, making better trains and laying more tracks was not going to save them. Redirecting their business to solve the basic customer need of getting people and materials from one place to another may have.

Define the business of the organization in terms of customer needs, not products and services. Consider customer needs and problems broadly to avoid missing market opportunities. Monitor market trends. Listen to customers. Continuously check for signs of denial (e.g., "no other product poses a competitive threat") and arrogance (e.g., "we make the standard") in the organization—they are sure signs that the organization is vulnerable to making strategic mistakes. Do not hesitate to engage in creative destruction, cannibalizing existing product lines to pursue new market opportunities.

Strategy

1.1.1

1.1.2 DO NOT MANAGE ORGANIZATIONS LIKE INVESTMENT PORTFOLIOS

Most managers are familiar with the investment portfolio strategy of risk management. A portfolio strategy involves diversifying investments so that negative conditions experienced with certain securities in a portfolio are offset by the positive conditions occurring with other securities. In lay terms, it is better not to put all of your eggs in the same basket.

Many managers assume that a similar approach is effective with regard to managing risk in organizations. For example, managers may seek to diversify product lines or target markets in order to smooth cash flow cycles or achieve stable growth. This assumption, however, is incorrect. The evidence suggests that internal diversification of this type is usually self-defeating, and more often than not it increases rather than decreases risk to the organization.

The reason is simple. Investors generally cannot actively participate in the management of organizations. Their only real lever for managing risk is portfolio diversification. Managers, however, have more powerful levers to influence an organization. They do not need to wait passively for good and bad things to happen—they have alternatives. And one of the best alternatives is to focus resources, not diversify them. An organization achieves the greatest reductions in risk by building competitive advantages and developing core competencies. This is not to say that organizations should never diversify. They should, however, diversify in a constrained manner that is consistent with and similar to their core business.

Strategy

1.1.2

1.1.3 MANAGE FOR THE LONG TERM—EVEN WHEN IT HURTS IN THE SHORT TERM

The pressure to trade short-term gain for long-term costs is often intense. Investors increasingly oust CEOs when they do not produce results quickly enough and reinforce CEOs who trade long-term interests for short-term interests. This latter situation has created a generation of executives who do what is necessary to achieve short-term goals and then leave the organization before the negative consequences of their actions are realized. The tyranny of the short term quickly permeates an organization.

When organizations have financial setbacks or share price decline, cutting production costs, downsizing, cutting pay, halting hiring, and eliminating training and development programs are often used as quick fixes to restore profitability and investor confidence. As a result, morale suffers, turnover of talented employees increases, and productivity decreases. There is little evidence that these kinds of short-term fixes actually fix anything. There is considerable evidence, however, that they do more harm than good in the long term.

No long-term success can be achieved without some short-term sacrifice. Resist the temptation to compromise long-term goals in light of short-term pressures, market fluctuations, or the effects of business cycles. Evaluate management performance based on the fundamentals of organizational performance: soundness of direction, effectiveness of execution, and productivity of people. Avoid management fads and other shortcuts to success. Such efforts consume time and resources and contribute little to the strategic health of the organization.

1.1.4 FAVOR OFFENSE OVER DEFENSE

Organizations that engage in more offensive actions than their competitors increase their probability of gaining market share and attaining market leadership. Offensive actions refer to proactive introductions of new pricing schemes, new products, and new promotions. Defensive actions refer to reactive changes in pricing, product, or promotional strategies and fortification strategies meant only to retain market share.

Offensive actions disrupt competitor strategies. This disruption results in a delay while competitors figure out how to respond, which in turn creates opportunities to seize market share. A steady stream of offensive actions keeps competitors on the defensive and gives the competitive advantage to the more offensive organization. For example, Nike executed three more offensive actions per year than Reebok from 1987 to 1990. In three years, Reebok sacrificed its 21-point market share advantage and the leadership position to Nike. Similarly, Microsoft took the leadership position in office productivity software away from Lotus, WordPerfect, and Computer Associates by executing more than 40 offensive actions per year than these competitors. Microsoft then widened the lead by increasing the number of offensive actions to well over 100 more than competitors.

The competitive advantage lies with the aggressor. Defensive strategies do little to retain market share or to preserve shareholder value over the long term. Develop innovative pricing, product, and promotional strategies and then quickly implement them. Do not wait for reactions from competitors before executing additional actions. It is preferable to execute a steady stream of new offensive actions to keep competitors off balance and on the defensive. Increased frequency and duration of offensive actions correlate with competitive advantage. However, increased complexity and unpredictability of offensive actions yield mixed results. The increased energy associated with managing increased complexity may offset any competitive advantage gained.

Strategy

1.1.4

1.1.5 RESPOND FASTER THAN COMPETITORS

The ability to respond to competitor actions faster than they can respond to your actions is a significant strategic advantage. The period of delay between observing an action and responding to an action corresponds to the potential for gaining market share and achieving market leadership. For example, it has been estimated that a market leader who responds more slowly than competitors by six months has about a 30 percent chance of losing its leadership position. The period, however, does not need to be six months. For example, one reason Tandy lost its leadership position to Circuit City is that Tandy took an average of 34 more days to respond than Circuit City. Similarly, Reebok lost its leadership position to Nike, responding an average of seven days slower than Nike.

Timing is important. For example, the element of surprise can dramatically increase the advantage for the aggressor by confusing competitors and delaying their time to respond. Fujifilm did exactly this to Kodak, using aggressive price cuts in anticipation of Kodak's annual discount program. The result was disruption of the Kodak strategy and a significant increase of market share for Fuji. In the battle for market leadership between Sears and Wal-Mart during the late 1980s, Wal-Mart consistently engaged in less predictable actions than Sears. Wal-Mart took away the leadership position from Sears in 1990 and continued to widen the gap throughout the 1990s.

Monitor competitor actions and react to them quickly. Consider developing rapid response teams to minimize the delay. Use surprise to disrupt competitor strategy and to increase their time to respond.

Strategy

1.1.5

1.1.6 USE THE COMPETITION AS A SOURCE OF FREE RESEARCH AND DEVELOPMENT

Strategy

1.1.6

"Good artists copy, great artists steal." This quote, generally attributed to Pablo Picasso, underscores a basic truth about innovation: it is hard. Innovation takes a long time, consumes large amounts of money and resources, and yields unpredictable results. It is much easier and less expensive to build on the work of others than to originate new products or business practices. For this reason, organizations should use the research and development efforts of competitors—in a legal manner.

Dell Computer exemplifies this practice. In an industry where investment in R&D ranges from 6 percent to 18 percent of revenues, Dell invests less than 2 percent. Dell typically cedes first mover status to competitors such as Sun, Apple, and Hewlett Packard, letting the market sort out which products will be successful. It then targets new product development on successful products, exploiting its low-cost operating model to underprice competitors. The result is minimal risk associated with market acceptance and minimal cost for R&D. This practice is not unique to Dell. Microsoft® Windows® was inspired by the Apple Macintosh, which was inspired by the Xerox Star. The strategy was employed by Japanese manufacturers with great success in the 1970s and 1980s. It is the basis for sharing organizational best practices. Successful organizations leverage the innovations of their competition in this way.

This is not to suggest that organizations should cease trying to innovate on their own. Rather, they should consider the innovations of their competitors as an additional resource for ideas, inspiration, and benchmarking. Successful research and development efforts are a function of knowledge of state-of-the-art products and practices as well as new lines of thinking. The activities of competitors are often the best source of the former and should be utilized as such.

1.1.7 EMBRACE MANAGEMENT FADS WITH CAUTION

Management fads change with the seasons. With the rise of each new management revolution comes the fall of three others. The problem for practitioners is discerning fad from substance.

Research indicates that there is no relationship between the adoption of management fads (e.g., empowerment, self-managed teams, TQM, 360-degree performance feedback, etc.) and a company's bottom-line financial performance. However, this is not to say that there are no benefits associated with such movements. A study of very large industrial firms found that organizations embracing popular management fads were more admired by the public and their employees were perceived to be more innovative.

Carefully review the costs and benefits associated with new management movements. Look at the evidence. Movements that promise quick fixes to complex problems should be looked upon with skepticism.

Strategy

1.1.7

1.1.8 ACT DIFFERENTLY THAN THE COMPETITION

There are two viable strategic positions for organizations: acting differently than the competition and acting more efficiently than the competition. Acting differently means doing things that competitors are not doing or doing things that competitors are doing but in substantively different ways. Acting more efficiently means doing things similarly to competitors, but doing them better—e.g., fewer defects, faster production, and lower costs.

Organizations that act differently than the competition generally achieve and sustain higher profitability than organizations that act more efficiently. A strategy based on difference provides value through the uniqueness of the offering. As a result, strategies based on difference are not cost-based. They enable higher unit prices and greater profitability. By contrast, a strategy based on efficiency provides value through the price of the offering. Strategies based on efficiency require unit pricing that is competitive with the lowest-priced competitor. Profit margins are smaller and tend to diminish quickly. Additionally, techniques for achieving efficiency are more easily copied. This means that advantages attained through efficiency of operations are short-lived.

To be successful, organizations need strategies that involve both difference and efficiency. However, the primary focus of strategies intended to provide long-term growth and profitability should be difference. Therefore, develop strategic positions that entail acting differently than the competition. Consider how easily the strategy can be copied and favor strategies that best preserve difference over time.

1.1.9 GROW THE CORE BUSINESS. PHASE OUT NONCORE BUSINESS

Organizations are often faced with tempting opportunities to delve into company investments or acquisitions that bear little or no resemblance to their core business. The best course is to defy temptation. Stay focused on the core business. To the extent that noncore business functions currently exist, phase them out.

Consider the actions of former Kimberly-Clark CEO Darwin Smith. Making paper products for magazines and writing pads had been the core business of Kimberly-Clark for over 100 years. When Smith focused the core business to consumer paper products only (e.g., tissues and diapers), he began phasing out the noncore business units—including the paper mill in the company's namesake town of Kimberly, Wisconsin. The move was hugely unpopular and was derided by analysts, shareholders, and managers of the company. However, the focus on the core business paid off. After 25 years, Kimberly-Clark became the world leader of consumer paper products and returned shareholder value at four times the market average.

Organizations have finite resources. Therefore, those resources must be used in a way that maximizes the probability that the organization can achieve leadership in a market segment or niche. Clearly define and grow the core business. Focus organizational resources on it. Phase out noncore businesses.

Strategy

1.1.9

1.1.10 OUTSOURCE NONCORE BUSINESS FUNCTIONS ONLY

It is a manager bias, if not charge, to constantly seek methods to reduce costs. Given the potential of outsourcing to achieve cost reductions, it is no surprise that outsourcing is increasingly considered an operational method of first choice to achieve more for less. However, despite its potential, the costs of outsourcing done improperly can easily outweigh the benefits. In fact, the evidence suggests that most outsourcing efforts—as high a rate as 75 percent—fail to meet expectations.

The reasons for this are many, but the most serious among them is the outsourcing of core business functions. Outsourcing core business functions not only exposes an organization to extreme short-term risk (e.g., the vendor goes out of business), but also compromises an organization's long-term viability by eroding its core competency. This erosion is often referred to as the hollowing effect.

The temptation to outsource core business functions is great. They typically constitute a large percentage of internal costs. Outsourcing agencies, especially those in third-world countries, often provide these functions at a fraction of the cost with the promise of comparable or superior performance. Despite this promise, organizations that outsource core business functions expose their core competencies to the competition, handicap the continued development of these competencies internally, and frequently discover that the reality of cost savings and performance gains is more elusive than the promise.

Therefore, avoid outsourcing core business functions. Typically, these are functions that are unique, difficult to copy, detrimental to be without, and closely related to the core competency of an organization. Consider outsourcing noncore business functions with caution. The potential of outsourcing is great—but rarely as great as the expectation managers have for it.

1.1.11 CONSULT WITH KEY PEOPLE IN THE ORGANIZATION WHEN CREATING STRATEGIC PLANS

There are three reasons for gathering input from people throughout an organization when creating a strategic plan.

First, organizational knowledge resides at all levels of the firm. Frontline or customer-facing staff often have insights into product or service performance that is not otherwise available. Managers in middle layers often detect inefficiencies in organizational processes, controls, and communications long before they become problems. Listening to these groups as part of the strategic planning process ensures that the plan is more accurate and complete.

Second, including people from throughout the organization in the strategic planning process softens the inevitable resistance to change. People are less resistant to change when they have a role—even a minor one—in helping to create the change. By actively soliciting input into the strategic planning process, planners can make the job of implementing the plan far less difficult.

Third, it is important to create prepared minds in management—i.e., to ensure that key managers have a thorough understanding of the business, share a common fact base, and agree on important assumptions.

1.1.12 REGULARLY REVISIT, REVIEW, AND REVISE STRATEGIC PLANS

Strategic plans are often written and then forgotten—used only on the rare occasion when someone inquires as to whether such a plan exists. This common mistake of "writing and filing" the strategic plan leads to a discounting of the goals set in the plan, as well as the legitimacy of all planning processes in the organization. Worse, since the existing plan was neither consulted nor followed, it becomes more difficult to recruit people to participate in future planning exercises. People come to view such exercises as "purely academic," with no real impact on organizational goals or performance.

To bring about true strategic change, strategic planning must be a continuous process. It cannot be a one-time event. Organizations that are committed to staying competitive must meet at regular intervals to rechallenge assumptions about the strategic direction of the organization and update and adjust the plan as appropriate. The world is constantly changing. The plan and the organization need to be prepared to change with it.

Approach strategic planning as a continuous process. Establish and maintain a regular meeting schedule with rotating participants to revisit, review, and revise the strategic plan. This ensures that participants understand the strategic positioning of the organization, refreshes thinking and perspective by involving new participants, and keeps the organization focused on its strategic goals.

Strategy

1.1.12

1.1.13 INCORPORATE MULTIPLE SCENARIOS AND CONTINGENCIES IN STRATEGIC PLANS

Despite recent criticisms to the contrary, research indicates that strategic planning is a worthwhile exercise for organizations. Organizations that engage in strategic planning tend to have higher rates of growth and profitability than those that do not. This is true for both small and large organizations, but the effects are strongest for large organizations. The benefit of strategic plans is twofold: promote adaptive thinking and increase the level of focus and integration of the organization.

Critics charge that the environment is too volatile for any predetermined plan to be successful. The result is a rigid plan that promotes a dysfunctional focus in times requiring flexibility, not rigidity. This criticism is valid for strategic plans that focus on one possible future. However, it is not valid for strategic plans that incorporate contingencies and scenarios. Strategic plans that incorporate these elements are far more effective at fostering adaptive thinking and are able to prepare an organization both psychologically and logistically for scenarios requiring change.

Consider the following actions when developing strategic plans:

- Develop a baseline plan based on a probable set of future events.
- Identify events within the baseline plan that have a high degree of uncertainty and/or the greatest impact on the organization.
- Develop detailed response plans for events that could bring significant harm to the organization. Define explicit "trigger events" to activate the response plans.
- Develop scenarios by exploring different chain reactions of events. These should be rich in detail and storylike in structure—the goal is to develop adaptive big-picture thinking, not to predict the future.
- Avoid "analysis paralysis" and focus planning efforts by limiting the number of events to no more than ten and the number of scenarios to no more than five.
- Meet periodically to review and update the plan.

1.1.14 APPLY THE 4+2 FORMULA

Organizations that excel at four primary management practices (strategy, execution, culture and structure) and two of any four secondary management practices (talent, innovation, leadership, and alliances) consistently outperform their industry peers.

Specifics within these management practices matter less than the practices themselves. For example, there is no indication that specific management techniques (e.g., TQM, Six Sigma) or technologies (e.g., CRM, ERP) matter that much. What matters is sustained commitment to using whatever approach or technology in accordance with the practices below:

4 Primary Management Practices (all 4 are critical for success)

Strategy   Organization has a clear, focused value proposition that combines a deep understanding of customer needs with a realistic assessment of internal capabilities.

Execution   Organization maintains operational excellence that achieves double the average productivity of general industries (i.e., 6% or more).

Culture   Organization fosters an environment that supports and rewards achievement and ethical behavior, and holds employees responsible for success.

Structure   Organization continuously seeks to shed unnecessary bureaucracy, extra layers of management, and outdated rules and regulations.

4 Secondary Management Practices (any 2 of 4 are critical for success)

Talent   Organization develops and retains talent through competitive compensation and training; favors internal promotion over external hires.

Innovation Organization aggressively pursues industry-transforming breakthroughs in methods and products.

Leadership Organization has a CEO that is perceived as an employee rather than an autocratic master; has ability to quickly identify problems and opportunities.

Alliances   Organization continuously seeks growth through mergers and partnerships.

Institutionalize the four primary management practices. Identify the two secondary management practices that best align with the organization, and formalize their adoption. Note that there is no significant benefit in trying to apply more than two of the four secondary management practices.

1.1.15 DO NOT HESITATE TO CANNIBALIZE EXISTING PRODUCTS

The economist Joseph Schumpeter introduced the concept of "creative destruction" in 1939. Schumpeter claimed that innovation is the driving force behind growth in a capitalist economy. Innovators contribute to economic growth by developing new offerings and selling them at premium prices, while imitators contribute to economic growth by copying these innovations and increasing competition. Profit margins fall as competition increases, which then set the stage for innovators to again create new offerings that can command premium pricing.

The implication of creative destruction for managers is that organizations should not hesitate to introduce new offerings that compete with its own existing offerings—even if the existing offerings are still selling well. Research indicates that organizations that continuously innovate and "cannibalize" their offerings in this way outperform organizations that incrementally innovate or wait until their sales begin to decline.

For example, Schering-Plough actively converts its prescription medications into lower-priced, over-the-counter versions, which quickly displaces the originals. Sales of their over-the-counter drugs typically double or triple as a result. Gillette has aggressively innovated and cannibalized its razor technology for over 30 years. The Atra, introduced in 1977, cannibalized its Trac II technology that was introduced in 1971. The Sensor technology, introduced in 1990, further cannibalized Trac II and began cannibalizing the Atra. The Sensor Excel technology was introduced in 1994, cannibalized the Atra and Sensor. And so the trend continues today. Home Depot is also a known cannibal, frequently opening competing outlets near existing stores if they are so busy that they are unable to maintain their standards of customer service.

Invest in research and development as an ongoing activity. Monitor the product development activities of competitors and continuously assess customer readiness for new products. Strive to beat competitors to market with offerings that compete with your own. Foster a culture that will cannibalize offerings without hesitation. To paraphrase a line by David Kilpatrick in his *Fortune* article, "Intel Goes for Broke," the goal for organizations should be to own the leading edge and share the trailing edge.

Strategy

1.1.15

1.2.1 CULTIVATE A QUIET AND FOCUSED LEADERSHIP CULTURE

It is widely believed that charismatic, heroic, and hard-charging leaders are responsible for making organizations successful. These leaders are typically characterized as passionate, courageous, and perpetually impatient and dissatisfied. Despite the popularity of this belief, less aggressive, less visible, and more contemplative leadership is more productive and effective.

Quiet leaders, as they are called, stay behind the scenes and out of the spotlight. They project a value system that is focused, committed, and constructive. Instead of using aggressive, forceful tactics, quiet leaders favor facilitation and collaboration. They are more concerned about making correct decisions than making popular decisions. Quiet leaders convey the fact that character, style, and approach should all point to performance excellence. They engender honesty, creative compromise, and patience in their staffs.

Not surprisingly, the benefits of quiet leadership have been difficult to detect—such leaders, by definition, avoid publicity. The visibility of such leaders dramatically increased once researchers evaluated leadership based on the long-term financial performance of organizations. The results of the research are unambiguous: quiet leadership outperforms other leadership styles. While their "louder" counterparts were holding press conferences and making commercials, the quiet leaders were working with their staff to make their organizations successful.

Educate managers about quiet leadership. Recognize and reward the practice in the organization.

1.2.2 FOCUS ON THE CRITICAL 20 PERCENT WHEN MAKING DECISIONS

Most decisions in organizations do not use formal processes or methods. In many cases, decision-making situations do not permit the formality or time required to use a more structured approach. However, use of the Pareto principle—also known as the 80/20 rule—is an accepted method for significantly improving the quality of decisions without adding to the time or complexity required to make the decisions.

The Pareto principle asserts that a small percentage of causes are responsible for a large percentage of the effect in a ratio of approximately 80:20. For example, 80 percent of the use of a product will involve 20 percent of the products features, 80 percent of the revenue comes from 20 percent of a company's products, 80 percent of innovation comes from 20 percent of the people, 80 percent of progress comes from 20 percent of the effort, 80 percent of errors are caused by 20 percent of the components, etc.

The implication of the Pareto principle is simple: managers should identify the critical 20 percent of the variables in any decision and focus time, attention, and resources primarily on that 20 percent. Effort applied to the right 20 percent can solve 80 percent of the problems. By contrast, effort applied elsewhere can solve only 20 percent of the problems. Significant change cannot occur unless it includes the critical 20 percent.

Use the Pareto principle in both tactical and strategic decision making. Use it to prioritize the decisions that are most important and then to focus resources on the critical variables of those decisions. The Pareto principle will reduce the time and energy required to make complex decisions and yield a higher probability of achieving a desired result.

1.2.3

1.2.3 COMMUNICATE LONG-TERM GOALS IN PERSON

Up to 70 percent of business strategies fail to achieve implementation. One reason this failure rate is so high is the poor manner in which long-term goals and strategies are typically communicated to organizations: not at all or using information-poor channels. The former is usually the result of concerns of what may happen if strategic information is inadvertently disclosed to competitors or of how the goals are likely to affect morale (e.g., a major strategic shift may signal layoffs). The latter is the result of convenience. The use of information-rich channels (e.g., speaking to someone in person) requires significant amounts of time and energy. It is more convenient to simply send e-mails or pass messages down through the chain of command.

Research indicates that strategic goals are more readily accepted and have a higher probability of success when employees understand the goals and the thought behind them. Concerns about competitive disclosure or the impact of the goals on morale are generally secondary considerations, since failing to achieve the goals in the first place renders these concerns moot. Additionally, strategic goals that are delivered in person by the CEO have a significantly higher probability of acceptance and success than delivery by other methods. In-person delivery is an information-rich channel of communication, permitting the opportunity to witness body language, ask questions, and share concerns.

Proactively share long-term goals with the organization. The CEO or other top managers in the organization should brief key staff in person—and the entire organization when possible. When organizations are large or geographically stratified, consider using "town hall" meetings or teleconferencing. The ability to receive and respond to feedback is critical to the success of these interactions. Provide ample opportunity for questions and discussion.

1.2.4 WANDER AROUND

Management by wandering around, or MBWA, is a term coined by Hewlett-Packard executives in the 1970s. MBWA is the practice of wandering around an organization, asking questions and listening to people. It ensures that executives get accurate information regarding the frontline challenges of the organization, and it builds trust between executives and employees.

The goal of MBWA is to improve communication. Wandering around provides opportunities for impromptu discussions, coffee talks, lunch meetings, and general networking. Recommended practices for MBWA include the following:

- Ask people to show you how they do their work.
- Ask for suggestions on how things can be improved.
- Remain open to any questions and concerns that are raised.
- Spend most of your time listening—not talking.
- Be a visitor, not a supervisor.
- Make visits spontaneous and unplanned.
- Give all areas of the organization near equal time.
- Act relaxed. People will reflect your feelings and actions.

MBWA is most effective when it achieves a frequency that renders it inconspicuous. This reduces the spectacle of the visit and increases the likelihood of open communication. Consider increasing MBWA following a major change that has created stress or hardship or to recognize, congratulate, or console a particular person or group.

1.2.5 CREATE A PERSONAL "ANTICIPATION REGISTRY"

Leadership

1.2.5

All organizations have an installed base of ideas that define the managerial mind-set, and this installed base is difficult to overcome. Senior executives stubbornly hold on to existing "playbooks," despite sometimes-obvious changes that have rendered the ideas obsolete.

When the leadership of organizations is unwilling to adapt to change, the leadership is effectively dissolved. Described by one knowledgeable observer as displaying a "fortress mentality, cut off from reality," Motorola is a classic example of this. In refusing to accept digital phones as the rightful and immediate replacement for analog phones, Motorola made a crucial error that led to its fall in the cellular market in the late 1990s.

In hindsight, former Motorola CEO Robert Galvin suggests the following process for executives: Each executive should keep an "anticipation registry" that records his or her insights on how the market is changing and what he or she is doing about it. While not all ideas will be good ones, the practice of keeping score (particularly if tied to compensation) is an important discipline.

1.2.6 CREATE A SENSE OF HEALTHY URGENCY

A sense of urgency is necessary for optimal productivity. If a sense of urgency is absent, employees will lack motivation. If a sense of urgency is too great, employees will experience excessive stress. Optimal productivity is achieved when a balance, or healthy urgency, between these extremes is achieved.

The most effective way to achieve healthy urgency is to communicate goals clearly, link the goals to specific persons or groups, and then explain why the goals must be met. It is important to present this case honestly; otherwise a "crying wolf" mentality will emerge in the company, productivity and morale will suffer, and future critical goals will not receive the attention they require. Risk taking and contrarian thinking should be encouraged to achieve the goals, but controls and support systems should be put in place to minimize the probability and consequences of failure.

Too little urgency creates complacency. Too much urgency creates stress. Complacency and stress are symptoms of an incorrect balance of urgency. Both reduce productivity. Managers should constantly gauge the environment for these symptoms and make the adjustments necessary to maintain healthy urgency and optimal productivity.

Leadership

1.2.6

1.2.7 APPLY POLICIES CONSISTENTLY TO ALL LEVELS OF MANAGEMENT

When policies are inconsistently applied to different levels of management within an organization, organizational justice is compromised. This results in a form of classism within the organization that undermines employee trust, unity, loyalty, and peak performance.

A common example of this is found when executives receive lavish increases in compensation while other levels of the organization are downsized or have their compensation reduced. For example, in 2002, Northwest Airlines significantly increased the compensation packages of their top two executives while announcing significant layoffs and lobbying for wage and work rule concessions from their labor unions. Despite the fact that the Northwest executives had compensation packages that were low relative to executives at competing airlines, the inconsistency of increasing their compensation at a time when the rest of the organization was being asked to make sacrifices did little to advance organizational performance or long-term shareholder value. Northwest Airlines was not alone. Similar compensation inconsistencies were revealed at American Airlines, Delta Airlines, and others.

Optimal organizations develop fair policies and administrate them consistently. No person in the organization should be "above" or "below" these policies. The only circumstance in which inconsistency may be preferable is when higher levels of management are held to a higher standard—not a lower standard—due to their increased visibility and responsibility. This punctuates the importance of the policy and the commitment of the organization to enforce it. It also gives the leadership of an organization the credibility to make changes by "walking the talk."

Leadership

1.2.7

1.2.8 SET CHALLENGING BUT ATTAINABLE GOALS

Performance is highest when employees are given specific, challenging goals versus vague, easy goals. Goals that are too difficult or unachievable, however, have the opposite effect. Setting specific challenging goals leads to higher performance than setting no goals or setting a general goal such as "do your best."

For goal setting to work, three conditions must exist:

1. Employees must be committed to their goals. This is achieved by ensuring that employees believe the goals are attainable and important.
2. Employees must receive constant feedback relaying progress in relation to the goal.
3. Employees must have (or develop) effective action plans for attaining their goals.

Goals can be set for any controllable behavior or outcome, including innovation. If the tasks leading to the goals are new or complex, it is preferable to assign learning goals rather than performance goals. This allows employees to focus on gaining the necessary expertise performing the task. Whether goals are set for individuals, teams, or departments, they should be consistent with company goals, competitive strategy, and ethical practices. They should not conflict with goals elsewhere in the company.

1.2.9 FAVOR REDUCING BARRIERS OVER INCREASING PRESSURE

Change occurs either by applying pressure on a system or by reducing opposing or restraining forces on a system. Applying pressure tends to increase tension on the system—whether the system is a person, a group, or an organization—intensifying the stress throughout. Reducing restraining forces on or in the system, by contrast, achieves change by increasing efficiency and lessening the total level of system tension. Given the costs and risks of increased stress, it is generally preferable to favor the reduction of restraining forces over increasing pressure.

Consider the initiative launched by Jack Welch at General Electric in the late eighties and early nineties called "Work-Out." The initiative focused on reducing restraints and barriers to effective performance and productivity. As Welch put it, "Work-Out meant just what the words implied: taking unnecessary work out of the system." Employee groups of 40 to 100 were asked to identify business and bureaucratic procedures that got in their way, such activities as reports, measurements, approvals, etc. Welch described these employee group meetings as follows:

A typical Work-Out lasted two to three days. It started with a presentation by the manager who might issue a challenge or outline a broad agenda and then leave. Without the boss present and with a facilitator to grease the discussions, employees were asked to list problems, debate solutions, and be prepared to sell their ideas when the boss returned. The neutral outside facilitator, one of two dozen academics, made the exchanges between the employees and the manager go a lot easier.

The real novelty here was that we insisted managers make on-the-spot decisions on each proposal. They were expected to give a yes-or-no decision on at least 75 percent of the ideas. If a decision couldn't be made on the spot, there was an agreed-upon date for a decision. No one could bury the proposals. As people saw their ideas getting instantly implemented, it became a true bureaucracy buster.

To improve the performance of systems, favor removing barriers and reducing restraining forces as the method of first resort. Change of this type incurs less risk of introducing new problems than increasing pressure, and the results tend to be longer lived.

1.2.10 ACTIVELY SUPPORT TRAINING AND DEVELOPMENT

Research indicates that the success of training and development programs in an organization depends largely on the degree that these programs are supported by management. In the absence of active management support, the most effective training and development programs will return little, other than frustrated employees likely to take their new skills to other organizations. High-performance organizations invest in training and development, make their investment and commitment to training known to employees, and then back words with actions by supporting employees in developing their capabilities.

Strategies to provide active support for training and development include the following:

- Be involved as a trainer, content provider, or participant.
- Recruit employees with particular areas of expertise to conduct internal training sessions. Attend these sessions to learn about and to support the effort.
- Allow adjustments to work schedules and provide help on work buildup when employees return.
- Encourage employees who have attended training to share knowledge with others through debriefings and informal teaching sessions.
- Recognize and reward employees who participate in training and successfully apply what they have learned to their job.

1.2.11 DECLARE A REVOLUTION WHEN RADICAL CHANGE IS REQUIRED

Leadership

1.2.11

Executives often perceive the need to implement change in short time frames. As a result, they often declare a revolution and implement sweeping, dramatic changes throughout the organization. This degree of change in a short period of time puts organizations at tremendous risk and should be considered a method of change of last resort. Generally, organizations can change more quickly and effectively by building on and redirecting existing systems and institutions. It is easier and more cost beneficial to redirect the momentum of existing systems than to eliminate them, replace them, and then work to regain momentum.

However, on rare occasions, revolutions are necessary. When the strategic positioning of an organization is threatened by an inability to adapt to changing market conditions and less drastic approaches have failed, revolution may be the only option. When this is the case, three key strategies for successfully achieving revolutionary change should be considered:

- Remove prerevolutionary leaders. The need for revolution indicates failed leadership. Those responsible for creating this need should be removed, or the revolution will lack credibility.
- Leverage middle managers. Middle managers dramatically affect the prospects for success of radical change. They typically have entrepreneurial ideas for change, have knowledge of and access to the internal social networks of the organization, are aware of changes in morale and individual emotional needs, and can moderate the effects of mistakes and extreme actions by upper management. Getting middle managers behind change efforts will largely determine success or failure.
- Hire consultants to help. Consultants can provide valuable positive external energy to facilitate organizational change. In addition to offering outside expertise, consultants can provide employees with an objective perspective on the changes that are occurring, helping employees cross the emotional bridge from the past to the future.

1.2.12 AVOID THE PRINCIPAL-PRINCIPAL PROBLEM

CEO stock ownership is good to a point. However, when CEOs become dominant shareholders, there is a real risk that their personal preferences will take precedence over what is best for the company. This is known as the principal-principal problem.

In many companies, the gap between ownership and control is minimal. There is a break point beyond which the healthy alignment of managerial interests with shareholders is compromised. When a CEO becomes the dominant shareholder, this break point is exceeded. The principal-principal problem occurs when the usual benefits realized from the incentive alignment between CEOs and shareholders are undermined by an overconcentration of power with the CEO. Rather than being a formula for reducing value-destroying initiatives and strategies, a CEO who is the dominant shareholder can lead to disaster.

A perfect example of this principal-principal problem is Samsung's misguided entry into the automobile business. The leadership of CEO Kun-Hun Lee was so strong that executives at Samsung were unwilling to challenge his decision. What makes this case so interesting is that Lee, the primary shareholder, is also the primary manager—a combination that is supposed to ensure superior decision making and value maximization. However, when there is no real countervailing force to a CEO, individual preferences can dominate. As an active manager and the largest shareholder of the company, Lee wielded extreme power that enabled him to quickly dismiss organizational resistance and bypass conventional protocols in decision making. These actions ultimately cost Samsung more than $3 billion.

1.2.13 CREATE SYNERGIES IN MERGERS AND ACQUISITIONS

Synergies are a combination of assets that create more value together than separate—usually from cost savings or revenue enhancements. From Boeing using McDonnell's underutilized lines and tool-making capacity when those companies merged in 1997 to Eaton's consolidation of plants and products following its acquisition of Westinghouse's Distribution and Controls business in 1994, cost synergies are essential to the strategic logic of a deal.

While virtually all acquisitions are predicated on realizing cost or revenue synergies, realizing these synergies is quite another matter. The first lesson is that synergies are often more difficult to realize than they appear. When synergy potential is modest, as it might be when two companies share few activities or customers, achieving these benefits is relatively straightforward. As synergy potential grows, the complexity of achieving synergy increases.

The second lesson is that along with this complexity, executives sometimes forget how much time counts in creating synergies. Synergies in the form of cost savings that materialize three years after an acquisition represent a different value than synergies that result in immediate savings. When promises made at the time a merger is finalized turn out to be considerably less robust over time, the market exacts a price—something AOL Time Warner learned when the pledge of a $1 billion boost to cash flow never materialized.

The final lesson is that creating synergies costs. Expenses usually include those from downsizing, time spent on coordination, additional training costs, and higher overhead during integration. A rule of thumb is that the one-time costs of synergy realization generally come in at two to three times the annual synergy benefits—i.e., the payback takes two to three years to exceed the costs.

1.2.14 DOWNSIZE IN ONE DRAMATIC EVENT—NOT GRADUALLY

Downsizing imposes financial and psychological costs on everybody in an organization. It should be the cost-cutting alternative of last resort. In the event that alternatives have been exhausted and downsizing of staff is still necessary, downsizing is best done in one dramatic reduction.

An American Management Association survey suggests that morale, productivity, and quality of customer relations diminish considerably after a downsizing. The beneficial effects of downsizing, such as reduced costs, improvements in quality, and increases in productivity, often take nine months or more to realize. A gradual approach to downsizing prolongs the negative and delays the positive.

Therefore, after all other cost-reduction methods have been attempted and have failed, downsize in one dramatic event. The organization will suffer less and recover more quickly.

Governance

Leadership

1.2.15

1.2.15 USE MORAL MANAGEMENT AS THE PRIMARY LEADERSHIP APPROACH

As the corporate scandals of 2001–2002 in the United States demonstrate, the costs of unethical leadership are high. For this reason, managers should adopt "moral" leadership as their primary approach. The criteria for *Business Ethics* magazine's annual ethics awards provide a practical definition of "moral management." Common features of the winner include:

- Being a leader in the company's field, showing the way ethically.
- Sponsoring programs or initiatives in ethical responsibility that demonstrate sincerity and ongoing vibrancy and that reach deep into the company.
- Being a significant presence so that the company's ethical behavior sends a loud signal.
- Standing out in at least one area—a company need not be perfect in all areas.
- Demonstrating the ability to face a recent challenge and to overcome it with integrity.

Moral managers:

- Conform to a high standard of ethical behavior.
- Adhere to accepted professional standards of conduct.
- Display ethical leadership.
- Want to succeed, but only within the confines of sound ethical precepts (fairness, justice, and due process).
- Justify right action on the basis of commonly accepted ethical principles, such as justice, rights, and utilitarianism.
- Obey both the letter and the spirit of the law.
- Strive to operate well above the minimal level that the law mandates.

1.2.16 USE COACHING TO ENHANCE EXECUTIVE PERFORMANCE

Coaching is a one-on-one relationship between a coach and an executive with the purpose of improving the executive's professional performance and personal satisfaction. Coaching addresses the inability of many executives to get people to provide them with honest advice, feedback, and counsel. Though coaching is a relatively new type of intervention, similar to but distinct from counseling interventions, there is suggestive evidence that it is effective at improving short-term performance and at facilitating change and that it is generally viewed favorably by managers. Its long-term benefits, however, are questionable. Additionally, coaching is not effective for executives who suffer from more serious psychological disorders (e.g., narcissistic personality), and in many cases, coaching a person with such a disorder can make a bad situation worse.

Strategies for maximizing the benefits of coaching include the following:

- Consider a psychiatric evaluation prior to coaching. Coaching can exacerbate existing psychological disorders. It is important to seek a psychiatric consult prior to coaching if there is any indication of psychological problems.
- Agree on roles and responsibilities. Both the coach and the executive must take responsibility for achieving change. These responsibilities should be defined and agreed upon.
- Define the problems collaboratively. Defining the problems is often an exploratory process. Until this exploration yields a consensus on what the problem is, it is pointless to discuss solutions.
- Define clear, measurable goals to address these problems. Define goals that are clear, measurable, and achievable within a reasonable period of time.
- Capitalize on moments of crisis. Crises are powerful learning opportunities. Most leaders refer to one or two key crises in their careers that were instrumental to their growth and success. When such crises exist, they should be used to drive positive change.
- Agree on a clear exit plan once goals are accomplished. Coaching should not continue indefinitely. Developing an exit plan at the beginning will facilitate moving through the life cycle of the process and guard against the development of dependency in the relationship.

1.2.17 BE EMPATHETIC

Being empathetic means to acknowledge and understand problems from the perspective of another. It is a significant factor in the ability to communicate and build trust effectively. Managers who are empathetic to the problems of employees build more effective employee relationships, foster more open and honest communication, and engender greater respect and loyalty among employees. Additionally, empathetic behaviors are critical to calming emotionally charged situations and diffusing conflicts. Empathetic behavior promotes helping behaviors and cooperation in organizations and is positively related to organizational performance.

Strategies for improving empathetic behaviors include the following:

- Listen carefully. Listen patiently and intently to what people say. Try not to interrupt or finish sentences.
- Ask open-ended questions. Ask questions that allow people to fully explore and explain their thoughts and feelings.
- Be nonjudgmental. Do not judge people or emotionally react to what they say. Passive acknowledgment does not mean agreement or acceptance.
- Use appropriate body language. Maintain eye contact and use facial expressions and body language that tend to mirror the communicator (e.g., smile when they smile, frown when they frown).

1.2.18 EXPLAIN THE REASONS BEHIND DECISIONS HONESTLY

Decisions that affect the interests, needs, and careers of individual employees are often extremely difficult to make and explain. For example, a manager may need to decide which employee out of a group of qualified employees receives a promotion. The decision of whom to promote is difficult enough; deciding how to explain the decision to other employees can be even more difficult.

Difficult decisions such as these lead many managers to distance themselves from the situation, fearing that they will be blamed for the decision or that their attempts at an explanation will make a bad situation worse. Some managers also believe that an explanation exposes them to litigation. Managers who believe this often give explanations that are feeble and incomplete, fearing that accidental mention of some detail will expose them or their organization to litigation.

The evidence, however, does not support these beliefs. In fact, providing honest and complete explanations for decisions reduces the likelihood of retaliatory behaviors by more than 40 percent. Additionally, research indicates that a failure to provide any explanation (or an adequate explanation) is far worse than simply explaining the reasons behind decisions honestly. Failure to adequately explain controversial or unfavorable decisions results in decreased levels of cooperation; increased levels of retaliatory behavior such as theft, work sabotage, and work slowdowns; and increased levels of absenteeism and turnover.

Explain the reasons behind decisions openly and honestly. Formalize the inclusion of explanations in decision-making processes. When presenting explanations, focus on honestly presenting the circumstances and reasoning that led to the decision. Avoid engaging in debate over subjective aspects or details of the decision.

1.2.19 FOCUS ON MEETING (NOT EXCEEDING) CUSTOMER EXPECTATIONS

That organizations should seek to exceed the expectations of their customers has become an unquestioned maxim. Research indicates, however, that this maxim is not only incorrect; it can be counter-productive.

Organizational resources are finite. Allocating resources to exceed customer expectations is done at the expense of addressing other needs in the organization—for a result that often goes unrecognized and unrewarded by customers. Leading companies rarely exceed the expectations of their customers, unless such a level of service is fundamental to their value proposition. Leading companies do, however, understand and meet the expectations of their customers. There are rarely negative consequences for failing to exceed expectations. By contrast, failing to meet customer expectations inevitably leads to significant negative consequence. Additionally, organizations need only achieve rankings in the top third of perceived quality in its industry to be successful. Higher rankings within this top third yields diminishing returns. The point is summarized nicely by William Joyce, Nitin Nohria, and Bruce Roberson: "the downside of poor quality is much greater than the upside of great quality."

Set standards of product quality and service based on a clear understanding of customer expectations. Do not seek to exceed these expectations, nor attempt to achieve perfection in meeting them. Once customer expectations are clearly defined and understood, go to those lengths necessary to meet these expectations to a standard of excellence within the top third of industry rankings.

1.3.1 ENSURE THAT A MAJORITY OF DIRECTORS COME FROM OUTSIDE THE ORGANIZATION

Directors are supposed to act in the best interests of the organization and not seek to receive undue benefits for themselves. However, boards consisting of the CEO, top managers, and close associates of the organization have inadequate supervision to ensure this mission. Therefore, a majority of the board should consist of outsiders.

The Sarbanes-Oxley Act, the SEC, and the stock exchanges have all established audit committee independence standards. Similarly, the IRS has set a standard for the board's compensation committee. Unfortunately, their definitions of "independence" vary greatly. Independence of the board can be gauged to some degree by asking and answering questions such as these:

1. Is the director consulting for the firm?
2. How often does the director publicly challenge the CEO or chairperson of the board?
3. Are there third-party connections between the director and the firm?
4. Does the firm make contributions to director charities?
5. Does the director hold share options in the company?
6. Does the board meet without the CEO or chairman present? If so, how often?

A board requires sufficient independence to properly serve the interests of the organization and its shareholders. A majority of outside directors on the board is the simplest and most powerful method for achieving this objective.

1.3.2 FOCUS ON OVERSIGHT AND NOT MICROMANAGEMENT

The board of directors is charged with overseeing the operations of an organization. As such, the board should focus on directing, encouraging, and leading, and not on the day-to-day problems that managers routinely handle.

Some boards, however, feel a need to control every action, issue, and problem in the organization. This micromanagement by directors results in increased interference, confusion, and disruption of operations. When a board steps in and takes charge, it makes managers wonder, "Is this my role, or is the board responsible for this activity?"

A micromanaging board:

- Wants to control.
- Lacks trust in the work and performance of others.
- Refuses to delegate.

This inability to rely on others (executives, managers, and nonmanagers) contributes to a failure to develop teamwork and generally creates discontent, cynicism, and high rates of turnover. Take measures to ensure that such micromanagement does not occur. Directors should conduct a periodic survey to determine whether they are perceived to be an oversight or a micromanaging group—and adjust their actions accordingly.

1.3.3 DEVELOP FORMAL CODES OF CONDUCT THAT AFFIRM ETHICAL VALUES AND BEHAVIOR

Organizations should openly affirm a commitment to appropriate ethical standards and make a sincere effort to implement them throughout their operations.

A formal code of conduct evidences such a commitment and provides a framework for implementation. Although development and publication of a formal code does not, in itself, constitute or guarantee ethical behavior, it is an explicit reminder of the organization's intentions and a reference point for dealing with specific situations.

The broad guidelines embodied in published codes should be augmented with memoranda dealing with specific topics, such as the giving and receiving of gifts and relationships with government officials. These published guidelines should be regularly followed up with workshops and training sessions for both employees and executives.

Governance

1.3.3

1.3.4 OBSERVE A ZERO TOLERANCE POLICY REGARDING DISCRIMINATION

Managers should make it clear on a regular basis that discrimination will not be tolerated in the organization in any form for any reason. Instituting this policy not only strengthens the perception of social justice in the organization, but also reduces risk of legal liability.

The Federal Equal Employment Opportunity Commission (EEOC) is the primary federal agency involved with enforcing Title VII of the Civil Rights Act of 1964, which prohibits discrimination in the workplace. The EEOC is an avid enforcer of the Civil Rights Act and readily comes to the aid of workers who file a legitimate claim. Organizations that have communicated and enforced a zero tolerance policy are less likely to be held liable for discriminatory actions than those who have not enforced such a policy. While it is impossible to police every action of every employee, an organization can simply and inexpensively develop and promulgate a zero tolerance policy.

Implementation of a zero tolerance policy should include the following actions:

- Develop a policy and create the means to enforce it.
- Engage independent counsel to review and sign off on the policy.
- Communicate the policy to everyone in the organization.
- Provide annual training to employees on appropriate workplace behaviors.
- Document that employees have received, understood, and agree to the policy.
- Enforce the policy in a firm, visible manner in the organization.

Governance

1.3.4

1.3.5 INSTITUTE A FORMAL PROCESS OF EVALUATING BOARD PERFORMANCE

Although 70 percent of the largest U.S. companies evaluate the firm's CEO, only about 33 percent evaluate the performance of the board of directors and only 20 percent evaluate individual directors.

Formal evaluation of board members generally results in the board as a whole attempting to improve the way it operates and individual directors striving to improve their individual performance.

The most effective board of director evaluations are:

- Conducted at least once a year.
- Started at the beginning of the firm's fiscal year.
- Established so the entire board defines and identifies the evaluation goals, process, and expectations.
- Limited to addressing a few crucial areas. Too many areas create difficulties in establishing priorities.
- Designed to obtain data and information from outside the firm (e.g., investors, suppliers, major customers, and regulatory bodies). External stakeholders can provide a different perspective than inside sources.

Following these guidelines benefits individual directors, the board as a team, managers, stockholders, and other stakeholders of the firm.

1.3.6 INSTITUTE A FORMAL PROCESS OF EVALUATING ORGANIZATIONAL PERFORMANCE

For organizations to maintain and improve their competitive advantage, performance must be tracked and measured over short and long time periods. Traditional organizational performance measures are inappropriate because they are:

- Based on cost systems.
- Not incorporated into strategy.
- Difficult to implement.
- Inflexible.
- Neglectful of customer requirements.

In 1990, the Nolan Norton Institute, led by Norton and Kaplan, introduced a comprehensive measurement framework called the "balanced scorecard." Designed to help communicate and implement an organization's overall strategy, balanced scorecards contain key financial and nonfinancial measures that are appropriate for the company's individual business units. Balanced scorecards ensure that the nonfinancial aspects of an organization are properly monitored and considered and focus attention on the key variables.

Use a balanced scorecard in tracking and evaluating company performance. Identify 10 to 20 key measures, such as profitability, customer satisfaction, internal business processes, and learning. The board's role is to oversee the development of the balanced scorecards; to use the scorecards to evaluate performance of the organization; and to ensure that the focus and performance of the organization is aligned with its mission, strategy, and culture.

Governance

1.3.6

1.3.7 APPOINT AN AUDIT COMMITTEE COMPRISED OF INDEPENDENT DIRECTORS

The U.S. government's reaction to corporate scandals involving Enron, WorldCom, Global Crossing, Tyco, and others was to pass the Accounting Industry Reform Act of 2002 (the Sarbanes-Oxley Act). This Act is designed to ensure that all members of a board's audit committee are entirely independent from the management of the company.

Audit committee members are considered independent if, from the date of their appointment to the committee:

1. They have not accepted, either directly or indirectly, any consulting, advisory, or other compensatory fee from the issue (company), or any of its subsidiaries (apart from fees of board service, including service on a board committee), and
2. They are not affiliated persons of the issuer or any of it subsidiaries.

To ensure compliance with the law, audit committees must be directly responsible for hiring, paying, overseeing, and (if necessary) dismissing independent auditors (not a director on the audit committee). The committee must have total independence from the organization's management and complete freedom to perform its duties. There is an increasing demand that audit committee members also possess financial expertise.

Governance

1.3.7

1.3.8 ENABLE DIRECTORS TO HAVE ACCESS TO MANAGERS BELOW CEO LEVEL

Communication between board members and employees is often channeled through the chief executive officer (CEO), which means that the board receives only information approved (or filtered) by the CEO. Boards should reject this "no contact" policy and demand access to any manager who can provide insight, ideas, and useful information.

Establishing such a "total access" policy requires that directors be allowed to talk to managers without consequences or hindrance. However, directors must accept that their communication efforts can be disruptive and expensive. Therefore, any contact system developed should be reasonable, fair, and mutually agreed upon by the board and the CEO.

Directors should also periodically sit in on management meetings. This may be awkward at first, but over time, managers will become comfortable with the directors and operate as usual. The directors can then observe, listen to, and become familiar with key managers. Provide managers with board members' e-mail addresses and telephone numbers to encourage open communication.

Governance

1.3.8

1.3.9 INSTITUTE A FORMAL COMPLIANCE PROGRAM

Recent high-profile fraud, deceit, and management malfeasance scandals have cast a light of distrust on the corporate world. Organizations can reduce the incidence of such misconduct and limit their financial exposure by developing a formal compliance program.

A formal compliance program is written and approved by the board of directors and is implemented by managers at all levels. The program should be designed to prevent, detect, and present corporate wrongdoing with respect to laws applicable to the firm, such as price fixing, bribery, collusion, discrimination, and safety.

A formal compliance program cannot stop all criminal activity, but it can reduce it. A formal compliance program is also a significant factor as to whether an organization should be prosecuted for the unlawful acts of its employees. And if an organization is convicted of a crime or found liable in a civil court, having a compliance program generally has a mitigating effect on criminal penalties and monetary fines.

The Organizational Sentencing Guidelines present the minimum requirements of a compliance program:

- Monitoring systems to discourage criminal behavior.
- Whistle-blowing process and policy.
- Disciplinary mechanisms to enforce compliance standards.
- Auditing process for the program.
- Steps to respond to and prevent similar instances of detected wrongdoing.
- Written documents.
- Communication system that includes all levels of employees.

1.3.10 ESTABLISH A RED-FLAG MONITORING PROGRAM

Governance

1.3.10

Monitoring red-flag issues such as performance, ethics, and legal compliance is a critical responsibility of an organization's board of directors. Therefore, senior management should be assigned the task of preparing a list of red-flag indicators for the board to review and consider. Once a final list is approved, it should become a standard part of the board's review material.

A responsibility of the board is to stay continuously informed. A board that relies solely on formal meetings to receive information is limited to remedial action. Therefore, directors need to install a reliable, open monitoring system that provides them immediate access to the critical performance, ethical, and legal measures. Common red-flag issues in need of monitoring include loss of key customers, resignation of key staff, failure to meet established organizational goals, significant problems of product quality or customer satisfaction, and any violations of legal or ethical standards of conduct.

Boards must also have clear and accurate communication channels that extend beyond the audit firm that provides financial information. Organizations such as Exxon have accomplished this by installing hotlines that employees can use to report problems they believe have occurred or are occurring. The board should actively head off problems by using these tools to monitor how management is making decisions, treating stakeholders, and conducting operations.

1.3.11 DISTRIBUTE BACKGROUND INFORMATION FOR UPCOMING BOARD MEETINGS IN ADVANCE

Before a scheduled board meeting, most directors are given meeting books that contain reports, legal opinions, spreadsheets, financial documents, letters, memos, e-mails, faxes, and graphs. Often directors receive these books the day before the meeting or as they enter the meeting room, which is an insufficient amount of time to review the information.

Although there is no standard definition of what constitutes "sufficient time" for review, some reasonable suggestions are as follows:

- Board books should be in the hands of board members at least two weeks in advance of the meeting. If additional important information is generated during this two-week period, it should be provided at the board meeting.
- Key financial, audit, and legal opinions should be in the front of the book.
- A limit as to how much goes into the board book should be established, with 100 pages being the upper limit.
- Board members should be encouraged to request additional information and data as needed.

Because reviewing, interpreting, and considering board books is one of the most crucial tasks of a board, directors should not allow review and analysis to be rushed.

Governance

1.3.11

1.3.12 LINK DIRECTOR COMPENSATION TO BOARD PERFORMANCE

Governance

1.3.12

Board members are generally paid a fee for their board service. Some firms offer additional forms of compensation, including retirement payments and stock-based compensation.

Corporate scandals, such as the Enron debacle, have put pressure on organizations to more closely link this compensation to board performance. There is a negative public image associated with excessive director compensation and a very real danger that directors focus on immediate stock price instead of long-term value.

Therefore, minimize base fees for board service and use compensation strategies that closely link director compensation to the performance of the organization. Research indicates that groups tend to perform at higher levels when they are evaluated and rewarded as a group. Use group-based compensation (e.g., stock-based awards to board members) when organizational goals are achieved versus individual compensation of director performance (e.g., meeting attendance).

1.3.13 PROVIDE STRATEGIC DIRECTION WHILE ALSO OVERSEEING STRATEGY IMPLEMENTATION

The most effective boards provide advice, opinions, and ideas that can help executives implement strategic plans. Boards do not form strategies themselves and should not become immersed in strategic-planning details or operating processes. By remaining free of details, the board can ponder, evaluate, and compare the positive and negative aspects of the strategic plan and the overall direction of the organization.

Even with effective board oversight, problems due to weak management practices, historical problems, inadequate development of key teams, successful competitor intrusions, and capture of market share can occur. Under these circumstances, the board should remain involved with strategic planning through the implementation phase. The board's job during this phase is to ask questions (and expect astute answers) about implementation progress, success, failure, key performance indicators, timing, and costs.

Using a thorough set of assessments to make judgments about implementation progress, the board should then evaluate the implementation progress, problems, and gaps of management. The board should recommend timely corrections, modifications, and extensions as necessary.

1.3.14 ESTABLISH A POLICY ADDRESSING WHISTLE-BLOWER PROTECTION

Most states offer whistle-blower protection, usually in the form of prohibitions against disciplining, discharging, or threatening to discipline an employee for blowing the whistle on inappropriate activities.

The board of directors, usually the audit committee, oversees the process by which employees can report alleged inappropriate activities. Therefore, the board should establish procedures for receiving employee complaints and any ethical, moral, and legal concerns in an anonymous and confidential manner. Further, employees should have confidential access to board members. Without a guarantee of confidentiality, no employee would have the requisite protection deemed necessary to disclose what he or she believes is improper activity.

The audit committee should also have the authority to engage independent legal counsel and other forms of advice, which is then paid for by the company.

Once a complaint is filed, the committee should appoint one director to handle and process it. An investigation should be conducted, appropriate corrective action taken, and the process documented.

Employees should be made to understand that disciplinary action will be taken if false accusations are filed. This is not intended to limit whistle blowing, but to emphasize the seriousness of making an allegation.

Once established, the whistle-blower policy should be circulated to all employees at least once each year.

Governance

1.3.14

1.3.15 APPOINT A NOMINATING COMMITTEE TO SCREEN AND SELECT DIRECTOR CANDIDATES

Finding, selecting, and retaining directors is an important process. The process must cover a wide array of factors, including the board's needs, teamwork dynamics, size efficiencies and concerns, and the availability of a diverse mix of competencies.

The recommended method of nominating, screening, and selecting new directors is through the creation of an independent nominating committee that is chaired by an outside director. The CEO should not be allowed to nominate or screen candidates or to participate on the nominating committee in any way. A CEO in this position possesses too much power.

Governance

1.3.15

1.3.16 LIMIT THE NUMBER OF BOARDS ON WHICH DIRECTORS CAN SERVE

Directors should be limited to serving on no more than two boards simultaneously. Without such a limitation, board members will find it difficult, if not impossible, to engage in the kinds of activities necessary to fully understand an organization's opportunities, strengths, weaknesses, and problems. This "two board" maximum rule ensures that the directors can give their full attention to the organization matters at hand.

It is not easy to find good director candidates. This shortage of talent becomes more problematic when limiting the number of boards on which a good director can serve simultaneously. Although a "two board" maximum rule restricts the director candidate pool, it is a responsible limit that helps to ensure director availability, participation, and focus.

Governance

1.3.16

1.3.17 ESTABLISH AND ENFORCE A MINIMUM LEVEL OF BOARD MEETING ATTENDANCE

Attending formal board meetings is one of the most important duties of a director. It is at these meetings that the board's business is conducted, that bonding with other directors occurs, and that important knowledge and experience about the organization is attained.

To maintain order on a board, mandatory meeting attendance should be required. The board chair has the responsibility of setting a minimum attendance limit and then making the rule known to all directors. Directors who violate the minimum attendance rule without due cause should be asked to resign from the board. In less extreme cases, directors should support the rule by individually expressing the importance of attendance to directors who miss meetings.

Governance

1.3.17

1.3.18 ESTABLISH AND MAINTAIN A CEO SUCCESSION PLAN

The board of directors must ensure strong, competent management of an organization. Therefore, succession planning is an area in which the board must take a direct interest. Succession considerations should be a board agenda item at least once annually.

A succession plan should include these important considerations:

- Strategic congruence—The succession plan must be consistent with the organization's strategy.
- Timing—A good succession plan anticipates the replacement of the CEO, whether expected or unexpected.
- Skills—Directors should understand the CEO's roles, responsibilities, and required skills and know which of these are needed to continue operating successfully.
- Assessment of talent—Regular assessment of homegrown talent should be a part of the plan.
- Firm's performance—The condition of the business should be monitored and recorded. In some cases, lack of performance is a reason to change CEOs.

Each organization is unique, but an established succession plan that is available and up to date allows change with minimal disruption. The plan should focus on the CEO, but extend to multiple layers of management.

1.3.19 PROVIDE CORPORATE GOVERNANCE POLICIES TO SHAREHOLDERS

The board's fiduciary and stewardship obligations should include keeping the owners knowledgeable. Governance policies on such issues as independence, oversight, evaluation, nomination, auditing processes, monitoring, and provision of counsel to the CEO should be made readily available to directors and the shareholders.

The board and management are tasked with running the company. Shareholders are not involved in operations or strategic planning. However, as owners, they have the right to know what the governance policies are and how they are being applied. Without access to corporate governance policies, shareholders do not know what questions to ask or by what standards to judge performance.

Communicating board policies opens communication, improves understanding, increases shareholder support, and minimizes adversarial conflict between directors and shareholders. In fact, shareholder review of corporate governance policies usually brings about an increased appreciation for the work and responsibilities of the board. Removing the mystique surrounding the board brings board members and shareholders closer together.

Governance

1.3.19

1.3.20 PROVIDE TRAINING FOR DIRECTORS

Directors who are knowledgeable about relevant industry trends, legal issues, environmental and economic factors, and competitors of an organization are true assets of their organization. Unfortunately, such directors are rare.

The knowledge and experience that typical directors bring to a board often do not overlap with the specific business of an organization. This hinders the ability of directors—especially outside directors—to evaluate decisions and challenge agendas advanced by dominant members or insiders. Without more specific knowledge of the organization's situation and challenges, these directors are handicapped in their ability to contribute meaningfully to the board and serve the organization.

Provide directors with the training necessary to understand the strategic challenges of the organization. Invite them to participate in operational meetings and to listen in on calls to customers. Encourage directors to attend seminars and conferences relevant to the organization.

1.3.20

1.3.21 ENSURE THAT DIRECTORS HAVE INPUT REGARDING BOARD AND COMMITTEE MEETING AGENDAS

A board that is dominated by one or more strong leaders may appear to be the most efficient. However, a few domineering directors can reduce the participation, commitment, and enthusiasm of the other directors. Ideally, the primary board leaders work at keeping directors focused and engaged in the entire range of board matters. They should not be allowed to run the board.

Therefore, ensure broad director participation and input by actively engaging directors to contribute agenda items prior to or at the beginning of board meetings. This enables all directors to substantively influence the work of the board. Additionally, consider balancing the influence of dominant board members through the use of committees. "Lead" directors rarely have time to be involved in all committees. Creating committees composed of different combinations of directors mitigates the influence of any one director and increases the contribution of other directors.

1.3.22 LIMIT THE NUMBER OF DIRECTORS TO BETWEEN 8 AND 14

The most effective boards have between 8 and 14 members. The average board has 11 directors. Small organizations often have boards of five or fewer directors. Large organizations often have boards in excess of 14 directors.

Small boards generally suffer a lack of representation, independence, and diversity of knowledge and experience. Large boards, by contrast, generally suffer a lack of productivity, cohesiveness, and commitment. Because there is often a limited amount of time to reach consensus, large boards mean that strategic issues are less likely to be sufficiently deliberated. These groups often splinter into smaller competing coalitions.

A rule of thumb is for small and medium-sized firms to have about 8 directors and larger firms to have about 14 directors.

1.3.22

1.3.23 APPOINT DIFFERENT PEOPLE AS CHAIRPERSON AND CEO

Combining the CEO and board chair positions is a widely used approach in many U.S. organizations. It is one of the primary enabling causes of the corporate scandals that occurred in the United States during 2001 and 2002.

The popularity of combining roles is based on the increased efficiency that comes with increased power. A single person acting as both CEO and chair has the enhanced ability to make and implement decisions more quickly. This is good when the decisions are good. This is bad—sometimes disastrous—when the decisions are bad.

It is precisely for this reason that the CEO and chair roles should be separated. Separate roles reduce the frequency of poor strategic decisions, conflicts of interest, and probability of groupthink and increase the probability of independent behavior on the part of directors. Separate roles empower the board to act with the proper structural tension between increasing shareholder value and protecting shareholder interests.

Corporate operations and leading human assets should remain the domain of the CEO. The board chair should be responsible for independent strategic thinking and corporate direction. One person appointed as both chair and CEO undermines the tension of "checks and balances" that keeps organizations healthy. It results in imbalanced governance and ultimately places organizations at undue risk.

Governance

1.3.23

1.3.24 ADJUST BOARD MEETING FREQUENCY TO MEET THE NEEDS OF THE ORGANIZATION

A standard board meeting schedule (e.g., quarterly) is good practice as long as it is subject to change when the organization needs more oversight and involvement. For example, in periods of crisis or imminent threat (e.g., cash flow problems, litigation, significant competitor activity), board meeting frequency should increase.

Research on the relationship between the level of board activity and financial performance suggests that organizations are more successful in years following increased levels of board activity (i.e., meeting frequency). However, publicly owned firms that increase their meeting frequency will suffer short-term devaluation in stock price—the market interprets the increased frequency as an indicator of problems. Thus, in publicly owned firms, directors should meet as often as necessary but not more often than necessary.

Adapt the board meeting schedule to meet the needs of the organization. Determine the next meeting interval at each meeting and adjust as necessary. In no case should a standard meeting schedule or director inconvenience take precedence over the immediate needs of the organization. Directors need to be able to adjust their schedules rapidly and attend meetings on short notice. This need for flexibility in attending impromptu board meetings should be a consideration when recruiting directors.

1.3.24

1.3.25 INTEGRATE STAKEHOLDER CONCERNS INTO THE MISSION AND PRACTICE OF THE ORGANIZATION

Over the past decade and a half, the stakeholder approach to management has surfaced as a way to achieve organizational objectives ethically. Relevant stakeholders include groups such as owners (shareholders), customers, employees, the community, and the natural environment, to name a few. To engage in stakeholder management effectively, management must answer five major questions:

1. Who are our stakeholders?
2. What are their stakes?
3. What opportunities and challenges do our stakeholders pose to the firm?
4. What responsibilities (economic, legal, ethical, and philanthropic) does the firm have to its stakeholders?
5. What strategies or actions should the firm take to best handle stakeholder challenges and opportunities?

Once these questions are answered, management should proactively acknowledge and work with the identified stakeholders. Consider The Timberland Company, the New Hampshire-based shoe and apparel company. It recently won one of *Business Ethics* magazine's Annual Business Ethics Awards. The award recognized Timberland for its effective stakeholder management with communities by establishing partnerships and volunteer relationships. One of Timberland's programs is Share Our Strength, one of the nation's leading antihunger, antipoverty organizations. Timberland's strategy is to promote its products while promoting a good cause; thus, the company and its community stakeholders are helped at the same time.

Proactive stakeholder management is good for a company and good for stakeholders. The alternative is to react when stakeholder interests are perceived to be compromised—an unpredictable and costly affair.

1.3.26 CONSIDER THE INTERESTS OF ALL STAKEHOLDERS—NOT JUST MANAGERS AND SHAREHOLDERS

The successful operation of any organization requires the approval and collaboration of numerous stakeholders. It is not necessary, and usually not desirable, for specific stakeholder groups to be formally represented on boards of directors. However, directors should adopt broad perspectives that address the diversity of stakeholder interests.

For example, individual or small groups of directors could be asked to represent the interests of particular stakeholder groups—employees, customers, local communities, etc.—and ensure that relevant issues concerning these groups receive proper attention from the board and from management. Actions by the organization that specifically affect particular stakeholder groups should be made known to those groups clearly and rapidly—and in advance, if possible.

Governance

1.3.26

2.0 EXECUTION

The ability to translate vision into consistent and concrete reality separates those who build substantial, lasting companies from mere visionaries. —Jim Collins and Jerry Porras

This section presents guidelines to help organizations achieve efficient execution through sound process, structure, and implementation. The ability to execute is as much mind-set as action. It involves continually asking how things can be done better, faster, and cheaper. It entails knowledge of how things are done elsewhere—not for the purposes of copying them, but for the purposes of transcending them. It means doing things differently than competitors and then doing them differently again when the competition copies you.

Consider Federal Express. FedEx is recognized around the world as the premier global provider of transportation, e-commerce, and supply chain management services. The FedEx family of companies includes Federal Express, Federal Express Ground, Federal Express Freight, Federal Express Custom Critical, Federal Express Trade Networks, and Federal Express Services. FedEx invented the air/ground express industry in 1971 in Memphis, Tennessee. The firm now operates in more than 210 countries and produces over $22 billion annually in sales revenue. More than 650 airplanes and 99,000 motorized vehicles deliver over 5.3 million shipments each day.

FedEx's dedication to efficient execution is highlighted foremost by its empowerment of employees to solve customers' problems. FedEx employees from the executive suite to the operating warehouses have the authority to take action when needed. If the customer has a problem, question, or concern, FedEx employees are expected to do what is needed to resolve the issue immediately. FedEx believes that traversing hierarchy is too time-consuming. Passing customer concerns from one layer to the next is not compatible with the FedEx culture. Decisions to correct problems and improve service are made at the point they occur. If a problem occurs in the distribution center, FedEx personnel have the go ahead to address it immediately. The empowerment of all FedEx employees is intended to be fast, efficient, and economical. Service to customers in real time is the FedEx norm.

FedEx has long maintained an advantage in execution through its mastery of technology. In the early years, Fred Smith, chairperson, president, and chief operating officer, insisted that FedEx own its transportation fleet. While competitors were buying space on commercial airlines and subcontracting their shipments to third parties, FedEx optimized its fleet and distribution system. When customers lacked the computing technology to take advantage of FedEx's new ordering and tracking technology, the company gave away more than 100,000 PCs loaded with its software to link and log customers into FedEx's system. FedEx was also the first organization to issue handheld scanners to its drivers, used to alert customers when packages were picked up and delivered. In 1994, FedEx became the first transportation company to launch a web site that included tracking and tracing capabilities. FedEx continuously sought ways to leverage new technologies to shorten processes, simplify structure, and streamline implementation. As a result, FedEx leapfrogged its competitors.

Those advantages, however, were short-lived. Competitors such as DHL, UPS, and TNT copied and enhanced many of these technologies and strategies. In response, Smith introduced a new FedEx strategy. He and the board created FedEx Ground (formerly RPS), FedEx Express (formerly Federal Express), FedEx Customs critical (formerly Roberts Express), and FedEx Logistics (formerly Caliber Logistics). Unfortunately, growth rates realized from this strategy did not meet expectations. As a result, FedEx reorganized operations to enable each group to function better independently and to compete collectively. The effort entailed a streamlining of functions and processes and a consolidation of sales, marketing, and customer service functions. This allowed customers to have one point of access to all groups, but preserved the unit level flexibility required for FedEx to remain competitive. The estimated cost of the reorganization was $100 million and three years.

Excellence of execution is a journey, not a destination. The guidelines in this section offer guidance for this journey. However, execution is as much about "doing" as "knowing." Execution requires not only a commitment to find out what does and does not work, but also a commitment to build on that knowledge faster than the competition. Execution is a continuous process of trial and discovery—occurring in the context of a race.

2.1.1 MEASURE PERFORMANCE IN SIMPLE, NONINTRUSIVE WAYS

The ability to measure performance accurately is essential to understanding and improving any system. However, selecting measures that are inappropriate in terms of quality or quantity is often worse than not measuring at all.

This is in stark contrast to the belief of many managers that it is preferable to have as much data as possible. The reasons for this belief range from a simple "more is better" philosophy to the desire for increased accountability to the belief that people perform better when they are being measured—whether or not the measures are used. Irrespective of the reasons, the belief itself is incorrect and costly to organizations.

When measures are too intrusive, they change the system being measured. When measures are too complex, they are vulnerable to interpretation and bias. When measures are too abundant, they dilute important data with unimportant data. Good measures provide data that provide insights and enable improvement. Bad measures provide data that muddle understanding and waste resources.

Use performance measures that are:

- Simple and meaningful.
- Resistant to bias and meddling.
- Few in number.
- Minimally intrusive—ideally, they are not even noticed.
- Focused on improving processes, not punishing people.

2.1.2 BUILD IN EVALUATIVE GUIDEPOSTS FOR NEW VENTURES WITH LONG-TIME HORIZONS

Pearl S. Buck wrote in *What America Means to Me*, "Every great mistake has a halfway moment, a split second when it can be recalled and perhaps remedied." This is particularly true for ventures with long concept-to-development times. These ventures often seem like good investments. However, by the time the products come to market, the competitive and organizational landscapes have usually changed significantly.

One approach to this problem is to evaluate these ventures with predetermined formal guideposts. When these evaluations yield results that do not meet specific performance and market viability criteria, define "exit ramps" to cut losses and abandon the project.

This is exactly what Boeing did late in 2002 when it canceled the Sonic Cruiser after the much-admired aircraft garnered rave reviews but no orders. For such a strong engineering company as Boeing, who was locked in a battle with Airbus, this could not have been an easy decision. It was, however, the right decision. It saved Boeing billions of dollars in a post-9/11 high-risk environment.

Boeing created an "exit ramp" option early in the development process. This allowed Boeing to continuously evaluate the product viability of the sonic Cruiser over its long development cycle. It also enabled Boeing to avoid unnecessary expenditures, as well as the psychological pitfalls of the "fantasy" product that can so easily emerge during a lengthy development phase.

Before ventures with long time horizons get under way, create specific guideposts in the project plan in which the entire project is evaluated. Make subsequent investments contingent upon meeting predetermined metrics at each guidepost. When guidepost metrics are not satisfactorily met, define "exit ramps" to abandon the project in the most cost-effective way possible. Such "exit ramps" strengthen the business plan and help keep sunk costs sunk.

2.1.3 ASSIGN A REPRESENTATIVE GROUP TO MAKE DECISIONS WHEN "BUY-IN" IS KEY

Group decisions generally achieve greater acceptance among represented parties than decisions made by a single person. Therefore, it is preferable to have representative groups make decisions—especially when decisions are controversial or require large-scale acceptance to achieve success.

For optimal performance in these cases, assemble qualified, representative groups of 7 to 12 people. Require unanimous agreement from the group and avoid conflict-reducing techniques, such as majority vote and bargaining.

A number of social dynamics can arise in decision-making meetings that can seriously compromise the quality of decisions. Therefore, it is recommended that group decision-making meetings be managed by professional facilitators or by designated employees who have received training on how to manage these dynamics.

Process

2.1.3

2.1.4 ASSIGN AN INDIVIDUAL EXPERT TO MAKE DECISIONS WHEN EFFICIENCY IS KEY

Group decisions are typically superior to decisions made by average individual group members but fall short of the best individual member. Therefore, it is generally preferable, in terms of both quality and expediency, to have one acknowledged expert make decisions whenever efficiency is key.

There is also a practical benefit to making decisions as quickly as possible: quick decisions that are incorrect result in important lessons of what does and does not work, which afford the organization time to adjust; slow decisions that are correct benefit the organization, but at relatively higher cost; and slow decisions that are incorrect bear both the cost of the error and the time lost.

Process

2.1.4

2.1.5 DETERMINE THE PARTITIONABILITY OF TASKS BEFORE ADDING RESOURCES

When under a time deadline to complete a project, it is common practice to add people to a project team. The assumption is that having more people on a project team will finish the project earlier. This practice rarely works.

Most projects are a collection of tasks that are unpartitionable—i.e., the completion of tasks depends in some way on the completion of other tasks and the communication required between workers. For example, software design activities cannot be completed until a complete understanding and communication of customer requirements is achieved, and software-debugging activities cannot be completed until the software application has been completely developed.

The only time the person/time substitution can be made is when a project is partitionable—i.e., made up of tasks that are completely independent and require minimal communication between workers. For example, a telemarketing initiative with the objective of contacting 1,000 unique households can be shortened in duration by adding additional telemarketers because each telemarketer works independently.

Therefore, determine the partitionability of tasks before making decisions about resource allocation. By simply adding people to a typical project, the project manager is increasing the cost, the complexity, and the time required to complete the project.

Process

2.1.5

2.1.6 RITUALIZE THE PRACTICE OF PROJECT DEBRIEFINGS AND SELF-EVALUATION

Project debriefings and self-evaluations should be conducted before, during, and after projects.

Debriefings give individuals an opportunity to voice concerns, receive updated information, and develop relationships with team members and the project's clients. As these relationships develop, members and clients will be more forthcoming about dissatisfaction and problems.

Self-evaluation allows individuals to determine whether they have fulfilled their project obligations and to assess strengths and weaknesses. Self-evaluation helps reveal what could have been better, what parts of the project were misread, and what steps are necessary to improve.

Documenting these processes is important. It provides guidance for future projects and serves as a learning tool for current project participants.

Process

2.1.6

2.1.7 SCHEDULE A "HALFTIME" AT THE MIDPOINT OF PROJECTS

There is one point in deadline-driven projects when team members are most open to reviewing, critiquing, and revising team strategies and methods—the project's chronological midpoint. This is true regardless of the duration of the project or the nature of the tasks involved.

The reason is likely a combination of how people think about time-based activities—i.e., as having a beginning, a middle, and an end—and practical considerations regarding completing a project on time. Near the beginning of a project, teams are mobilizing. They make initial decisions about how to approach a project and are resistant to implementing changes before they have data about whether the approach will be successful. Near the end of a project, it is usually too late to make significant adjustments and still complete the project on time. The project midpoint is a natural point to pause and assess the effectiveness of the approaches used.

Therefore, formalize calling a "halftime" at the midpoint of projects. Use this time to ask tough questions about how project activities have been conducted and to honestly assess whether the project is on track to be completed on time. Note that team receptivity to this kind of self-evaluation is greatest at the midpoint, so non-critical feedback should be saved for the "halftime." Consider dividing large projects into multiple, smaller projects. This creates more midpoints, providing more points of intervention. When projects have no natural end point, consider creating artificial end points.

Process

2.1.7

2.1.8 KEEP WRITTEN COMMUNICATIONS SHORT AND SIMPLE

Managers today are inundated with information. The consequence is the dilution of relevant information with irrelevant information. Therefore, written communications must be short and simple. This improves both efficiency of communication and efficiency of thought. A memo sent by Sir Winston Churchill to the War Cabinet summarizes the point nicely:

To do our work, we all have to read a mass of papers. Nearly all of them are far too long. This wastes time, while energy has to be spent in looking for the essential points.

I ask my colleagues and their staff to see to it that their reports are shorter.

The aim should be reports which set out the main points in a series of short, crisp paragraphs.

If a report relies on detailed analysis of some complicated factors, or on statistics, these should be set out in an appendix.

Often the occasion is best met by submitting not a full-dress report, but an aide-memoire consisting of headings only, which can be expanded orally if needed.

Let us have an end of such phrases as these:

"It is also of importance to bear in mind the following considerations", or "Consideration should be given to the possibility of carrying into effect". Most of these woolly phrases are mere padding, which can be left out altogether, or replaced by a single word. Let us not shrink from using the short expressive phrase, even if it is conversational.

Reports drawn up on the lines I propose may first seem rough as compared with the flat surface of officialese jargon. But the saving in time will be great, while the discipline of setting out the real points concisely will prove an aid to clearer thinking.

2.1.9 COMMUNICATE IMPORTANT MESSAGES IN MULTIPLE WAYS

When messages are important or involve complex issues, use multiple channels of communication. Multiple channels are redundant, but this redundancy improves the probability that the important message will be received and understood.

Communication media differ in their information richness (i.e., the amount of information they can carry and the extent to which they enable senders and receivers to reach a common understanding). Media that are high in information richness are capable of transmitting more information and are more likely to generate a common understanding than media that are low in richness. Information richness of media from the highest to the lowest transmittal methods are face-to-face (highest), verbal-electronic transmittal, personally addressed written, and impersonal written (lowest).

The information richness of communication channels corresponds to their cost in time and energy; the more information rich the channel, the more time and energy required to communicate the message. Therefore, the cost benefit of the channel advantage must be weighed against the time and energy required to communicate the message.

Favor information-rich channels when the communication is critical or sensitive in nature, such as dealing with a customer complaint. Follow up with written correspondence to memorialize the event. Use information-poor channels for noncritical communications, especially when convenience and cost considerations are key.

Process

2.1.9

2.1.10 CREATE AND FOLLOW AN EXPLICIT AGENDA AT EVERY MEETING

Informal meetings frequently suffer a lack of structure and direction. They often start late, proceed inefficiently, and end before issues are resolved. Formalizing meetings by building an agenda is an effective method for increasing their productivity. Building an agenda at the beginning of a meeting allows all members to have their issues addressed, allows prioritization of agenda items when time is constrained, and focuses discussion on the business of the meeting.

Agendas should be:

- Developed and distributed before meetings, when possible.
- Developed (or updated) at the beginning of each meeting by team members.
- Reflective of the input of all team members.
- Prioritized by team members.
- Time-bounded by item when time is limited.
- Enforced by a team-appointed moderator.

Use agendas to improve the productivity of meetings. Ensure that all team members are invited to contribute agenda items. Once the agenda is finalized, follow it. Do not allow the activities of the meeting to lose focus. When additional items are realized during the meeting, add them if time permits. Otherwise, add the item to the agenda for the next meeting.

Process

2.1.10

2.1.11 DOCUMENT MEETING EVENTS AND ACTION ITEMS

Documenting meeting events and action items ensures clarity and understanding of commitments and expectations and enables all parties to have a record for follow-up meetings. The document becomes an informal contract that is a point of reference for both parties.

Effective documentation:

- Objectively states the key points of the meeting.
- Uses specific examples of key points.
- States concisely what is expected by a specific date.
- Identifies key milestones.
- Identifies when performance will be discussed again.
- Identifies what characteristics will be monitored.

The habit of documenting agreements emphasizes the importance of meetings. Additional benefits include increased focus, accountability, and legal protection. The practice of documenting is worth the time and effort.

Process

2.1.11

2.1.12 EXPLAIN WHY CHANGE IS NECESSARY BEFORE IMPLEMENTATION

Process

2.1.12

People need to be motivated toward and prepared for change. Even when change will clearly lead to an improved situation, people often do not embrace change unless they personally recognize the need to do so.

To accomplish this, people need to become dissatisfied with the way things are. They must see a gap between what is and what would be better. Sometimes this process is obvious and straightforward; for instance, sales have fallen dramatically or morale is exceptionally low. In other instances, the need for change may be less obvious. In these cases, the need must be articulated; that is, the gap between what is and what is more ideal must be defined and clearly presented. The case for change must be made. For example, the CEO of Pathway Stores had to communicate to the supermarket chain's 28,000 employees the need for change to avoid bankruptcy. To prepare them for change, the CEO prepared a video that spelled out in detail the financial debt, problems, and plans. Some employees quit, fearing the worst. However, the remaining 99-plus percent committed to do what was necessary to get the company back to health.

Gather facts about the current situation. Contrast the information with a goal state. The goal state may be an unfulfilled vision from the past or a newly defined vision for the future. Clearly illustrate the discrepancy between the current state and the goal state. The discrepancy creates an emotional and cognitive tension, helping people consider the change proposal with an open mind. Then make the case as to why the status quo is no longer viable. Explain how the goal state addresses the problems. People will see the difference between the actual and the desired and will experience a need to reduce the gap.

2.1.13 CLEARLY COMMUNICATE WHAT WILL AND WILL NOT CHANGE

An element of stability helps people cope with change. People better handle the chaos and complexity of organizational change when they know that some aspects of the organization (e.g., compensation package) will remain stable.

For example, in 1987, British Airways (BA) changed from a government-sponsored organization to a private corporation. This required a significant change in BA's strategy and culture. The leader who drove this change, Colin Marshall, emphasized the need to move from an engineering-driven culture to one that was more market-driven and customer-focused. This had many old-line managers and staff thinking that the "good" parts of the BA culture would be sacrificed. To persuade them that this was not the case, Marshall noted the engineering strengths that would be retained as well as the changes that would be needed to give BA a more customer- and market-focused orientation. This enabled a smoother cultural transition, which resulted in BA becoming one of the most profitable airlines in the industry.

When communicating change to an organization, avoid the temptation to emphasize only those things that will change. Give near equal time to the many things that will not change. This more accurately describes the whole nature of the initiative and prevents stress associated with not knowing the status of unmentioned items.

Process

2.1.13

2.1.14 DEVELOP AN EXIT STRATEGY FOR OUTSOURCING AGREEMENTS

The life of an outsourcing relationship usually ends before the life of the outsourcing organization. Therefore, it is necessary to plan in advance for the end of the outsourcing agreement, rather than trying to deal with the end when it comes. As basic as this planning seems, it is rarely done. It is unpleasant to negotiate the terms of separation at the same time a business relationship is being consummated. However, this is precisely the time that the exit strategy needs to be developed and the corresponding contract terms incorporated into the outsourcing agreement.

Outsourcing organizations should ensure that important business functions continue with minimal disruption in the event that the outsourcing agreement ends—e.g., the vendor goes out of business, breaches the agreement, or performs poorly. Much of the risk associated with outsourcing agreements can be minimized through contract terms that ensure reversibility and switching. Reversibility clauses secure the outsourcing organization's right to purchase equipment and hire employees. These clauses are generally used to minimize the consequences of a vendor going out of business, but are also used when the size of the agreement is large in scope or long in time. Switching clauses secure the outsourcing organization's right to receive assistance from the vendor to switch to another vendor or to internalize the service. These services usually include integration, procurement, and training support.

Develop exit strategies before signing outsourcing agreements. Secure the strategy using the appropriate contract terms in the outsourcing agreement. The absence of these terms not only exposes an organization to unnecessary risk, but also weakens the organization's ability to enforce existing terms and to negotiate new terms at the time of renewal.

Process

2.1.14

2.1.15 USE BENCHMARKING TO IMPROVE ORGANIZATIONAL PRACTICE

Although benchmarking was originally designed to focus on improving the quality of organizations, it has proven to be useful in pinpointing trends, performance gaps, strategic advantages and disadvantages, and best practices. Benchmarking is a process that involves learning from others. It is not a process of copying or duplicating what others are doing, but an approach that provides comparative information, data, and procedures. For example, in developing the Lexus, Toyota spent over $500 million on benchmarking its car and services with main competitors Mercedes and BMW. Toyota wanted to improve upon the competitors' cars and service by creating a superior vehicle.

The basic steps of benchmarking are as follows:

- Determine what to benchmark (e.g., salaries, work practices, or expenditures).
- Establish a benchmark team.
- Join with partners to share information.
- Collect and analyze data.
- Identify strategies to improve practice.
- Implement strategies.
- Evaluate changes and repeat the process.

Sharing meaningful comparative information allows managers to accurately assess and improve their ideas, concepts, and model. Attempting to benchmark too many factors often results in a lack of focus on the trends or ideas that are most important. Therefore, identify a few key variables that need to be benchmarked. Refrain from addressing every relevant factor.

2.1.16 SHARE EXPERIENCE AND BEST PRACTICES ACROSS BUSINESS UNITS

Process

2.1.16

Benchmarking with other organizations has received considerable attention as a means of dramatically improving the execution performance of an organization. By contrast, relatively little attention has been accorded the sharing of best practices within the organization. This is unfortunate since the benefits of sharing internal best practices are significant—perhaps more significant than benefits of external bench-marking. For example, Texas Instruments realized over $1.5 billion in annual free wafer fabrication capacity by transferring best practices among its fabrication plants. Similarly, Chevron's program of sharing ideas on energy use has saved the organization well over $650 million since its adoption. If sharing best practices within an organization represents these kinds of potential improvements, why aren't more organizations doing it? Simply put, sharing best practices is easier to achieve in theory than reality. A number of factors interfere with the successful transfer of best practices internally:

- Ignorance—People are simply unaware of practices elsewhere in the organization.
- Resource limitations—People do not have the time or resources to implement new practices.
- Weak relationships—Relationships between the source and the recipient are insufficient to enable the efficient transfer of information.
- Internal competition—People are unwilling to share knowledge because they compete internally with other groups for money, status, or resources.
- Time to implement—Transfer of best practices is a lengthy process, taking an average of 27 months to transfer from one part of an organization to another.

The benefits of sharing best practices internally are measurable and long-lasting. The challenges to realize these benefits are significant, but they can be overcome. Create opportunities to build and nurture lasting relationships across the organization. Such relationships are prerequisite for meaningfully sharing information. Consider developing best-practice teams to continuously explore and share practices in the organization. Cultivate a culture of sharing and changing, ensuring that compensation systems do not undermine the willingness to share information. Allow time for people to learn and change. Do not try to share everything at once. Identify the most critical areas of the organization and focus sharing efforts there first. Be patient. Change takes time.

2.1.17 ASSESS TRAINING NEEDS BEFORE IMPLEMENTING A TRAINING PROGRAM

A needs assessment serves as a foundation for training programs. The purpose of conducting needs assessments is to identify and prioritize training needs in the organization. The outcome of this assessment should be a prioritized list of specific competencies that link to job objectives (e.g., improve proficiency with a software package in order to reduce average production time). Three levels of analysis should be used to determine the training needs:

1. Organizational—Focuses on identifying where in the organization training is needed
2. Operational—Focuses on identifying the content of training or what the employee must do on the job to be considered or rated a high performer
3. Individual—Examines how well each employee is performing important job tasks

Training programs implemented without the benefit of a needs assessment rarely achieve measurable organizational results. Therefore, standardize the practice of conducting a needs assessment before implementing training programs. Identify the key competencies of the organization that can be improved through training. Prioritize training for those competencies, as they will yield the largest return for the training investment.

Process

2.1.17

2.1.18 STRIVE TO ELIMINATE ALL FORMS OF EXCESS AND WASTE

Minimizing excess and waste in an organization is a simple method of improving its efficiency and profitability. While such improvements cannot, by themselves, make an organization successful, they can make it more competitive. Consider, for example, Nexfor Inc., an international forest-products company. In the late 1990s, Nexfor launched a comprehensive cost-reduction program called the Margin Improvement program. Through an intensive combination of training, waste reduction, and sharing of internal best practices, Nexfor achieved $160 million in annual margin improvements. Nexfor's success is not atypical. Organizations tend to become less efficient as they grow, providing increasingly greater opportunities to realize savings through the pruning of excess and waste. Big or small, however, the benefits of such programs generally outweigh their costs.

Proven strategies to reduce excess and waste include the following:

- Simplify and standardize processes.
- Consolidate similar products.
- Eliminate redundant functions.
- Install cost controls.
- Avoid unnecessary measurement.
- Reduce hierarchy.
- Share best practices internally.
- Empower employees.
- Automate tasks when possible.

Do not allow the culture of an organization to become complacent regarding operational efficiency. It is the one aspect of an organization's success to which every employee can significantly contribute. Consider developing teams charged with identifying and removing excess and waste in the organization. Give them the responsibility and authority to achieve challenging goals in this regard. Insist on quick results. Cost-reduction initiatives usually fail when they require more than 12 months to yield results.

Process

2.1.18

2.2.1 SIMPLIFY SYSTEMS AND PROCEDURES

With rare exception, simpler systems perform better and more reliably than their more complex counterparts. Simple systems are easier to understand, maintain, and change. Their interactions with people and other systems are easier to predict, and they are easier to tune and refine over time.

Unfortunately, keeping systems simple is a challenging, continuous struggle. The natural tendency of all open systems is to become more complex with time. And complexity begets complexity. Organizations, for example, naturally become more bureaucratic as they grow because new staff, technology, policies, etc., are continuously being added to the old. These additions require additional support and maintenance, which in turn requires more staff, technology, policies, etc. Organizations become increasingly bloated and inefficient and are unable to respond to the competitive activities of smaller, more agile players.

This evolution toward increased complexity is best managed by a conscious, aggressive commitment to simplify the systems and procedures of an organization. The direct benefits of simplicity are generally quickly and visibly attained. The indirect benefits, however, can be even greater, though more difficult to detect. Unnecessary complexity often creates problems that ripple through an organization in unexpected ways. These problems often require actions that also have ripple effects, and so on. The simplest system to do a job will minimize these second- and third-order effects, dramatically increasing the efficiency of the organization.

Strategies to simplify systems and procedures include the following:

- Make policies short and simple.
- Flatten the hierarchy of the organization.
- Keep written communications short and meetings brief.
- Minimize the complexity of compensation and benefits.
- Push decision-making authority down into the organization.
- Use the minimum number of performance measures possible.
- Eliminate meaningless job titles and job category distinctions.
- Reduce the number of suppliers to the organization.
- Revise procedures to require the fewest actions possible.
- Review and refresh all of the above on a regular basis.

Structure

2.2.1

2.2.2 CENTRALIZE POLICY AND DECENTRALIZE MANAGEMENT

Many organizations cycle between periods of centralization and decentralization. When organizations are perceived to be unfocused, or inefficient due to redundancy, managers generally favor centralized command structures. The argument is that performance is best served through increased control and the elimination of redundancy and waste. When organizations are bureaucratic and slow moving, managers generally favor decentralized command structures. The argument is that performance is best served through increased decision-making authority by the people who are closest to the problems.

Generally, the optimal organizational structure is one in which decision-making power is decentralized, but guided and controlled by policy that is issued and enforced by a centralized authority. This allows the strategic focus and cost-control benefits of a centralized structure, as well as the agility and responsiveness of a decentralized structure.

Keys to successfully centralizing policy and decentralizing management include the following:

- Communicate policies clearly and widely.
- Hold managers accountable for achieving goals.
- Establish clear boundaries within which autonomy is encouraged.
- Replace hierarchy with self-managed teams.
- Encourage communication of best practices between units.

2.2.3 INSULATE RESEARCH AND DEVELOPMENT TEAMS FROM MARKET FEEDBACK AND INTERNAL POLITICS

A common belief in both research and development and product development circles is that the focus of their efforts should be customer-driven. This belief is, however, overly simple. Development efforts that are directed or influenced by customer feedback suffer from a kind of customer-based myopia, which limits the potential of development to the average vision of the customer base. This myopia is not necessarily harmful (in some cases, it is helpful) when the development focus is refining existing products. However, it is detrimental when the focus is developing innovative new products.

It is useful to distinguish between two types of product development: sustaining and disruptive. Sustaining development is incremental. It supports and refines existing technologies to meet generally recognized customer needs. Customers provide useful feedback in the development of sustaining technologies, appreciating their development because they address recognized needs. Disruptive development is revolutionary. It creates new market opportunities by redefining how things are done. Consequently, customers are able to offer little toward the development of disruptive technologies and such technologies are rarely adopted within existing markets.

Since most organizations try to be responsive to customer feedback, they often invest increasing amounts in sustaining technologies and decreasing amounts in disruptive technologies. As a result, internal political forces tend to mount against development of disruptive technologies in support of sustaining technologies. This keeps customers happy, but puts the organization at a strategic disadvantage. Competitors introducing innovative new products can completely disrupt the market. This happened to IBM, who remained fixated on mainframe computers while the minicomputer was being introduced. It happened to Digital Equipment Corporation, who remained fixated on the minicomputer while the desktop computer was being introduced. And it happened to Apple and Commodore, who remained fixated on the desktop computer while the portable computer was being introduced. In each case, market leadership was lost due to customer-based myopia and the introduction of disruptive technologies by competitors.

Market leadership is rarely gained or lost due to sustaining technologies. It is usually gained or lost due to disruptive technologies. Maintain research and development efforts on disruptive technologies. Insulate the research and development teams from market feedback and organizational politics—e.g., locating product development teams at remote locations and controlling lines of communication to those teams.

2.2.4 DESIGN JOBS THAT POSSESS HIGH-CORE JOB DIMENSIONS

Most jobs, whether managerial or nonmanagerial, possess five core dimensions that can be designed to be more challenging. The more "loaded" a job is in these areas, the more complex and preferable the job is to employees. High-core job dimensions reduce absenteeism, improve morale, and increase productivity.

The five core dimensions are:

1. Skill variety—the different activities, skills, and competencies needed.
2. Task identity—the completion of a whole or identifiable segment of work.
3. Task significance—the impact the job has on the lives or work of others.
4. Autonomy—the freedom, independence, and discretion a worker has to schedule work time, work flow, and task completion.
5. Feedback—direct, clear information about how well the jobholder is doing.

Determining the proper balance between these core dimensions is a crucial part of management. Favor combinations that closely match an employee's personality to preferred job dimensions (person/job fit). Good person/job fit results in higher levels of intrinsic motivation, which in turn increases employee performance and frees management resources.

2.2.5 PROVIDE EMPLOYEES WITH "WHOLE" TASKS

Employees should be given "whole tasks"—i.e., jobs in which they can participate from start to finish. This gives employees an understanding and appreciation of the big picture and their contribution to the larger mission of the organization. Working on whole tasks also increases productivity and quality. Whole tasks require fewer intermediate handoffs and the attendant time, errors, and misunderstandings that arise with such handoffs.

The concept of task wholeness has been embraced in many industries. In the auto industry, for example, an assembly team may build an entire car from start to finish. This concept not only provides task significance ("I build cars" versus "I install steering wheels"), it also permits workers to gain appreciation of the overall assembly process, offers opportunities for workers to improve the process, and improves the quality of the finished automobile.

Task wholeness works in service industries as well. In the insurance industry, for example, a claim processor might be responsible for all of the steps of the claims process rather than being a "form checker," who checks a single aspect of the claim and then forwards it to another employee for further processing.

Provide whole tasks to employees when possible. Employees involved in all of the steps of a process will be more motivated, less bored, and able to offer better service to customers.

2.2.6 SEPARATE RESPONSIBILITY FOR TASK COMPLETION FROM RESPONSIBILITY FOR TASK ASSISTANCE

As today's organizations attempt to increase the collaborative efforts of their workforce, they should encourage employees to embrace higher levels of cooperation, not penalize them for it. This "performance penalty" often arises when an experienced employee is asked to help a less experienced coworker complete a work assignment. Doing so makes the experienced employee responsible for the coworker's assignment, which serves as a disincentive for the expert and encourages abdication of responsibility in the coworker.

Consider this situation: An expert in computer systems performance was widely known for her abrasive style and opposition to working with others. During a conversation with an academic researcher, she lamented that the more she helped others, the more willing others were to offload their projects on her. In effect, the more she helped, the busier she became. Working alone was her way of managing workload, but it had the negative effect of limiting the help she provided to the organization.

The manager's job is to ensure that workers who need assistance from an expert maintain primary responsibility for task completion—regardless of whom they ask for help. Keeping responsibility and assistance separate improves the chances that local subject matter experts will be willing to help.

The principle of "offering help without taking responsibility for the problems of others" can help create an environment that is energized, collaborative, and powerful. Ignoring this principle can result in a decrease in cooperative effort and an increase in the phenomenon of sole contribution.

2.2.7 MAINTAIN AN UP-TO-DATE ORGANIZATIONAL CHART

Although current literature on organizational design encourages firms to break down barriers between departments, none suggest that departments or functions should no longer exist. It would be highly inefficient for organizations to operate without formal reporting lines, boundaries between functional units, and identified groups of individuals focused as one on a common goal. The very nature of the term *organization* suggests that people have been united in a common cause and have committed to acting on its behalf.

The organizational chart, though much maligned and often closely associated with that other pejorative term *bureaucracy*, is useful. The organizational chart is vital to understanding process flows and communication channels. It provides a "map" of the human resource terrain and can be a source of powerful insight into ways of improving organizational processes. Organizations should feel free to be innovative with their organizational chart, as long as its primary function is to identify reporting lines and functional boundaries.

Keep organizational charts up to date. Make them readily available to anyone within the organization who wants to examine them. Keep charts simple, reflecting the minimum level of detail possible. This simplicity will make them easier to maintain. Be sensitive to how business units and people are represented in the chart. For example, the position of a business unit in a top-down hierarchy is often interpreted to reflect its relative importance to the organization.

Structure

2.2.7

2.2.8 ACTIVELY SUPPORT TELECOMMUTING OR DO NOT USE IT AT ALL

Telecommuting is a work arrangement whereby employees work out of their homes regularly, generally using a computer and related telecommunication equipment.

Telecommuting reduces stress levels for workers, frees up time ordinarily spent commuting, and provides greater autonomy. It is a powerful and popular means of accommodating many of the work/life balance issues that confront employees today.

The primary problems of long-term or frequent telecommuting are isolation and disruption. These problems reduce communication and cultural participation with the on-site employees, increase the frequency of miscommunications, and often result in telecommuters receiving less consideration for participation and promotion.

The cost benefit of telecommuting is determined by how effectively management addresses those problems. Stay in contact with telecommuters. Be available to answer questions and concerns. This is more important for telecommuters than for on-site employees. Supply the necessary software, hardware, and technical support necessary to do the job. Organize schedules to ensure adequate communication and participation of telecommuters. If these commitments cannot be sustained, do not support telecommuting at all.

Structure

2.2.8

2.2.9 INSTITUTE FORMAL, DIRECT LINES OF COMMUNICATION BETWEEN EXECUTIVES AND EMPLOYEES

Organizational design should take into account communication flow between top officers and employees at all levels. Most organizations have multiple layers of management. These layers often prevent direct communication between an organization's top officers and employees several layers beneath them. These barriers prevent critical customer data from reaching key decision makers. These barriers also prevent critical interactions between decision makers and action takers that are vital to maintaining morale.

Employees at all levels should have an ability to communicate directly with top officers about issues and concerns they are experiencing in their organizational roles. Direct communication channels between employees and top officers often are not implemented because managers at interceding layers fear a loss of control. This fear is legitimate and must be addressed. Direct communication channels with top officers must allow people to address any matter, but the intention of the channel should be to address primarily strategic issues, such as:

- Patterns detected in organizational processes that belie inefficiencies or unnecessary costs.
- Customer feedback on product or service performance.
- Customer feedback on features of the product or service that are most/least attractive.
- Ideas or suggestions about organizational strategy and long-term plans.

Institute formal lines of communication to bridge communication gaps between different layers of the organization. An open-door policy is a start, but it is not adequate by itself. Multiple lines of communication should be considered, including e-mail, telephone hotline, bulletin board system, regularly scheduled small-group meetings, etc. Ensure that communications are primarily strategic in nature, but make allowances for circumstances regarding grievances, harassment, or other critical job-related matters. Install procedures to address managerial concerns of abuse of these channels by subordinates. Consequences for such abuse (e.g., reporting false information) should be severe. Protect the confidentiality of employees who provide feedback. Consider making at least one channel of communication anonymous so that the identities of employees who provide sensitive feedback are protected. However, consider feedback provided anonymously with caution.

2.3.1 SET DIRECTION ABOUT ENDS, BUT NOT MEANS

A common practice for managers is to focus on means rather than ends. This is a mistake. Managers should provide clear direction to teams about what they are expected to accomplish and the basic parameters within which they must work (e.g., timelines and budgets). Beyond this, managers should not specify the means for achieving goals; the team should determine how to achieve their goals. Conversely, teams should not be given the responsibility of determining their own goals. The democratic approach is not preferred here. Team goals should be defined by the manager and presented in a clear and unequivocal manner. Managers often feel uncomfortable about clearly and authoritatively presenting goals in this way. They often worry that a team will not embrace and own the goals or that the team will not be able to meet the goals necessary for success. The result is the defining of goals that are vague or the setting of less risky subgoals. These, too, are mistakes. Team performance is compromised when goals are perceived to be incomplete or inconsequential.

Provide clear, relevant goals for teams. The goals should encompass whole tasks and involve genuine risk of failure—there is no real sense of accomplishment without risk of failure. Clearly define controls for the team so that the operating limits are well defined. Then get out of the way and let the teams work.

2.3.2 KEEP TEAMS SMALL

Keep teams small. Team productivity is optimal when team size is about six, but productivity diminishes exponentially when team size is over ten. Ensure that the team membership is diverse—i.e., team members should have diverse views about how the work can best be done. Diversity increases task-related conflict on the team, but yields higher rates of productivity. Note that constructive task-related conflict is more important than interpersonal harmony for promoting team excellence.

Teams

2.3.2

2.3.3 KEEP TEAMS TOGETHER—THEY ONLY GET BETTER WITH TIME

Research indicates that group longevity significantly influences team effectiveness. Teams that stay together for long periods are better at understanding and respecting the roles of individual members, anticipating actions and reactions of members, responding to individual members' needs, and communicating effectively. On average, teams need about two years to achieve optimum performance levels.

Membership in productive teams should be kept stable. Switching members into and out of teams is disruptive, frustrating, and inefficient. Recruit and assign team members who are able to stay with the team for extended periods. Ensure that team membership is rewarded and that it does not hinder career advancement. When additions to teams are necessary, encourage team members to recruit qualified friends and colleagues. This facilitates integration and minimizes disruption.

Teams

2.3.3

2.3.4 ENSURE THAT NEW TEAMS REALIZE EARLY SUCCESS

The early success of new teams is requisite for their long-term success. Early successes build confidence in and cohesion between team members. New teams that experience early failures, by contrast, suffer significant problems of team trust and confidence. Early failures can irreparably harm team morale and perpetuate failure through the self-fulfilling belief that the team cannot perform.

The probability that new teams experiencing early success will have long-term success is far greater than for new teams experiencing early failure. Therefore, it is important to maximize the long-term success potential of teams by ensuring their early success. These early accomplishments become a powerful motivator for teams to take on increasingly challenging tasks and ultimately form the basis of a wider performance culture.

Set relatively modest goals for new teams. Support, guide, and coach team members through their initial projects. Recognize and celebrate team successes.

2.3.5 EMPHASIZE FAIRNESS

One of the most significant factors of high-performance teams is the degree to which team members perceive their treatment to be fair. Fair treatment and fair policies generate the best work cultures and team productivity. When treatment or polices are perceived as being unfair, team members do not work as hard, are less committed to the organization, and are less likely to be cooperative and helpful.

Factors that influence the perception of fairness of team members are as follows:

- Size—Perception of fairness is easier when teams are small.
- Diversity—Perception of fairness is more difficult when ethnic and gender diversity is high.
- Value congruence—Perception of fairness is easier when team members share common value systems.

Clearly, teams of different sizes, degrees of diversity, and value systems provide many important benefits. Understanding the key factors that influence the perception of fairness enables managers to anticipate and address problems before they occur.

Establish clear and fair policies. Treat people fairly and ensure that team members treat one another fairly. A primary cause of people perceiving that they are being treated unfairly is poor communication. Therefore, install communication and feedback systems—especially when teams are large or diverse. Emphasize the need for openness. Document important meetings and decisions to ensure clarity and understanding.

2.3.6 ENSURE THE CONTRIBUTION OF ALL TEAM MEMBERS

Social loafing is the tendency for certain group members to exert less individual effort in large groups. It occurs when people fail to take needed actions because they believe that others will take those actions.

To ensure optimal productivity and fairness, it is important to engage all group members in tasks. A simple and effective way to do this is to make the contributions of each group member visible. An old saying is "Many hands make light the work." A number of studies show that when overall group performance is publicly displayed, individual members tend to provide less effort. Conversely, when individual contributions to group performance are publicly displayed, individual effort of group members is maintained or increased.

Identify clear and fair measures of individual performance. Publish the results of these measures in a visible, appropriate location. Recognize and reward performance on these measures in such a way as to avoid alienation or embarrassment for relatively low performers. Ensure that the measures do not promote internal competition.

Teams

2.3.6

2.3.7 CREATE A WAR ROOM FOR PROJECTS REQUIRING HIGH LEVELS OF INTERACTION

The term *war room* refers to an office arrangement that allows people to see and overhear one another. This open design ensures that team members are exposed to problems and solutions, issues with other team members, and other organization-related information. The result is improved problem solving, communication, learning, team building, and productivity.

Research comparing the productivity of war rooms to traditional office arrangements (offices and cubicles) found that team productivity in war rooms was more than twice that of traditional arrangements—and continued to increase with time. Team members with no previous experience working in war rooms liked them better than expected and ended up preferring them to traditional arrangements. Concerns over the level of distraction were found to be less than expected. However, the war room arrangement did increase concerns among team members about individual recognition.

The primary benefit of war rooms is also a liability—ambient noise and lack of privacy. While team members develop the ability to tune out much of the noise, it is important to provide access to spaces where team members can address individual problems and private matters (e.g., study rooms and conference rooms). Install devices to facilitate shared communication, such as whiteboards, flip charts, and central worktables. Ensure mechanisms to recognize and reward extraordinary performance of individual team members.

2.3.8 FAVOR GROUP-BASED REWARDS OVER INDIVIDUAL-BASED REWARDS

Except in tasks where individual performance is clearly independent from the performance of other people or systems, group-based rewards should be favored over individual-based rewards.

Group-based rewards improve the performance of teams and individual team members. They increase team cohesion, morale, and the perception of fairness. Group-based rewards also increase the level of knowledge sharing and helping within the group. Individual-based rewards can improve the performance of individual team members, but they generally worsen the performance of the team. Individual-based rewards increase internal competition by reinforcing self-interested behavior over group-interested behavior. They decrease team cohesion, morale, and the perception of fairness.

Therefore, favor group-based rewards over individual based rewards. Group-based reward systems are most effective when:

- All members of the group are actively engaged and contributing.
- Rewards are shared equally by all group members.
- Clear procedures are in place to address the poor performance of individual members.
- Members receive the training and support necessary to be successful.
- The danger of regressing to the mean—high performers doing less; low performers not doing more—is openly discussed and guarded against.

Note that contingent-pay systems should be applied only to groups with a high willingness to take risks. Exempt employees tend to find such systems more motivational than nonexempt employees, as do employees at higher versus lower levels of an organization.

Teams

2.3.8

Teams

2.3.9

2.3.9 STRUCTURE COMMON TASKS AND SHARE REWARDS TO IMPROVE GROUP COHESION

Believing that a goal is either cooperative or competitive affects worker expectations and interaction. In cooperation, people believe that as one group moves toward goal attainment, others do as well. They want others to pursue their goals effectively because effectiveness helps everyone reach his or her goals.

Goals that are competitive imply that achieving one's goal makes it less likely that others will attain theirs. When one succeeds, others fail. These expectations restrict information and resource exchange, which frustrates productivity, intensifies stress, and lowers morale.

When Hartzell Manufacturing established an individual production incentive plan, employees bickered over what machines would allow them to get bonuses easier and refused to learn to operate less profitable machines. It was an "everyone for himself or herself" environment. Hartzell then switched to a factory-wide bonus program under which employees received base pay plus 50 percent of productivity increases, measured by more parts produced, reduced scrap, less rework, and fewer returned parts. The change was dramatic. Cooperation increased, product got out faster, and fewer parts came back. Employees better understood how the business operated, and Hartzell became a better place to work.

Common tasks and shared rewards catalyze group cooperation and enthusiasm. Groups operating in such an environment are more productive, are more efficient, and possess higher morale than groups using alternative task-incentive configurations.

3.0 PEOPLE

Executives should spend more time on managing people and making people decisions than on anything else. No other decisions are so long lasting in their consequence or so difficult to unmake. —*Peter Drucker*

This section presents guidelines to help organizations cultivate and retain talent. Realizing the untapped potential of people in an organization is usually the surest and least expensive method for improving bottom-line performance. It is also the least used method. The reasons for this are many, but likely stem from the widespread view that effective management equates essentially to effective control. Overcoming this classic myth of management is fundamental in realizing the full potential of the people in an organization.

Consider Southwest Airlines. In 1971, Southwest Airlines began flying with three aircraft serving Dallas, Houston, and San Antonio. Today the company has over 370 planes in its fleet. The airline employs 35,000 employees and has operating revenues of over $6 billion annually. It has achieved 30 years of profitability—a level of sustained profitability unheard of in the airline industry.

This growth is largely attributable to Southwest's public commitment to supporting and empowering its employees. A clear benefit of such a commitment is recruitment. Southwest receives over 100,000 job applicants a year. There is an emphasis on peer recruiting—pilots attract other pilots; flight attendants bring in other flight attendants. To further evaluate candidates for the right job fit, a thorough process is used. Applications, phone screenings, individual interviews, group interviews, and votes are used to find the best employees. The thoroughness, peer involvement, and large pools of candidates result in attracting those individuals who can perpetuate the Southwest culture and the organization's concern about people.

An important point is that there is nothing extraordinary about the compensation system at Southwest. Most people take a salary cut to work there. Southwest pays pilots and flight attendants by the trip. This results in compensation that is slightly lower than the industry average, but provides the flexibility to work more hours. Approximately 90 percent of all employees own stock in the company, with about 11 percent of Southwest's outstanding shares owned by employees. Executive-level compensation is modest. Turnover at Southwest is about 4 percent per year, or less than half that of other airlines.

In the early 1990s, Southwest renamed its human resource department the "People Department." The first job of the People Department was to throw away the 300-page corporate handbook. Individuals joining the department were required to have line experience. Employees are considered customers of the group. The motto of the People Department is presented on a large poster that states:

> *Recognizing that our people are the competitive advantage, we deliver the resources and services to prepare our people to be winners, to support the growth and profitability of the company, while preserving the values and special culture of Southwest Airlines.*

Given this commitment, it is not surprising that all Southwest employees attend training programs to emphasize customer service, teamwork, management practices, and open-book discussions of Southwest as a company. Internal development of employees is considered a priority. Colleen Barrett, the current president, started as former CEO Herb Kelleher's legal secretarial assistant. She is described as the main customer ambassador and is known as a stickler for detail and customer service. One of her favorite committees, which she chairs, is concerned only with sustaining Southwest's spirit and culture.

Fortune magazine consistently identifies Southwest as one of the top 10 businesses to work for in the United States and one of the most admired companies in the world. In 2002, *The Wall Street Journal* reported that Southwest ranked first among airlines for customer satisfaction according to a survey by the American Customer Satisfaction Index. *Business Ethics* listed Southwest in its "100 Best Corporate Citizens," a list that ranks public companies based on their corporate service to various stakeholder groups.

Southwest Airlines has found the formula for optimizing and sustaining performance. Many of the elements of this formula can be found in the guidelines in this section. Still others await discovery at companies like Southwest. One thing is certain: the power of an organization to adapt, perform, and grow is truly with its people.

3.1.1 HIRE INTERNALLY WHEN QUALIFIED CANDIDATES ARE AVAILABLE

The benefits of internal promotion generally outweigh the benefits of hiring outsiders. The only case in which hiring is preferred over the promotion of a qualified internal employee is when a radical shift in direction or thinking is required. Even in this instance, however, internal candidates who have demonstrated the capacity to lead and change should be strongly considered.

The benefits of internal promotion over outsiders are many:

1. Costs associated with internal promotion are lower than costs associated with identifying, qualifying, and hiring an outsider.
2. Compensation is, on average, less for internally promoted employees than for outsiders.
3. Time to productivity is significantly less for internally promoted employees than for outsiders.
4. Internal promotion cultivates greater morale and loyalty in the organization and reduces attrition.
5. Internal candidates are known quantities relative to outsiders and therefore constitute less risk.
6. Internal promotion tends to promote longer-term approaches to problems.

The risk of internal promotion is said to be the perpetuation of legacy thinking and operations. However, research does not support the view that outsiders remedy this more effectively than insiders. Therefore, favor internal candidates when they exist. Consider external hiring when internal alternatives have been exhausted.

Acquisition

3.1.1

3.1.2 IMPLEMENT A COWORKER REFERRAL PROGRAM

Acquisition

3.1.2

Hiring based on coworker referrals can result in cost savings on recruitment expenses such as advertising, job fairs, and commissions. Additionally, having a relationship with an existing employee provides instant socialization and support—the referred worker is likely to form positive relations with other employees with whom the referrer has relationships. Friends of the referring coworker are likely to help, support, and encourage the coworker's friend or acquaintance. For example, at Juniper Networks in Mountain View, California, employees are expected to refer at least one other person. Almost 90 percent of new hires at Juniper come via employee referrals.

Coworker referrals do, however, have negative aspects. In low-performing environments, coworker referrals often reproduce or encourage the status quo. Another risk is the increase in collusion among friends, which can result in conflict among and within groups.

Many organizations encourage employee referrals. It is assumed that current employees understand the qualities of the potential applicants, know the needs of the company, and are unlikely to refer someone whose performance would reflect badly on them. These assumptions are generally correct when the caliber of the referrer and culture is high. However, when individual or cultural performance problems exist, coworker referrals often compound these problems. Referrals should be used with particular caution when significant organizational change is required.

3.1.3 PROVIDE JOB CANDIDATES WITH A REALISTIC JOB PREVIEW

A realistic job preview (RJP) provides job applicants with positive and negative information about the job—without distortion or exaggeration. RJPs are relatively inexpensive to develop and implement, and they result in improved selection and reduced attrition. For example, A.G. Edwards & Sons gives every broker applicant a quick taste of reality. First, the applicant reads a booklet describing the first-year broker's life on the job—the challenges, hours, expectations, and average earnings. Then a private interview with a broker takes place to discuss day-to-day problems, satisfaction, and other realities. Finally, the applicant listens to a tape of customer-broker discussions, complaints, and difficult rejections.

A realistic job preview should present both positive and negative characteristics of the people, resources, culture, expectations, history, and compensation programs of the organization. The RJP should be objective, clearly presented, and specific in terms of details provided. Individuals exposed to RJPs have lower turnover rates and report higher job satisfaction than individuals exposed to only positive descriptions of jobs. By making candidates' expectations more realistic, employees are less likely to leave when confronted with negative conditions or situations.

Provide RJPs to applicants in person (versus, for example, a written description) and as early in the hiring process as possible. RJPs presented early are more effective because applicants have not expended significant time and effort that increases their commitment to taking the job.

Acquisition

3.1.3

3.1.4 USE PSYCHOMETRIC TOOLS AS GUIDES ONLY

There are many simplistic "assessment" and "team-building" tools on the market. These tools often lead managers to label people using various scoring methods or classification schemes. Such approaches generally result in unproductive, self-fulfilling prophecies that can be personally hurtful and highly counterproductive.

Simplistic assessments do not belong in professional work settings. Carefully research any assessment tool (and the company behind it) prior to implementation. Require evidence that the assessment can do what it claims.

Acquisition

3.1.4

3.1.5 CONSIDER GENERAL MENTAL ABILITY IN HIRING PRACTICES

When carefully implemented, "intelligence" is the single best predictor of long-term job performance. Job candidates who score well on such tests (i.e., general mental ability tests) are better able to handle emergencies, deal with time pressures, manage stress, solve problems, learn how to use new technologies properly, adapt to structural and personnel changes, and work effectively in a culturally diverse work group.

Despite the predictive power of general mental ability, managers have been reluctant to consider it in hiring processes. This is likely due to stereotypes about people who score well on such tests (e.g., they are socially inept, or they don't work well with others) or from the belief that there is little variance in intelligence among the candidates within a particular job category. In the former case, there is no evidence to suggest that such negative personality traits correlate with intelligence. In the latter case, there is evidence that significant variance exists within most job categories.

General mental ability tests are relatively low-cost, reliable indicators of future performance for most jobs. The tests have the potential for race and gender bias—but used with caution, they should be incorporated in the hiring process.

Acquisition

3.1.5

3.1.6 USE SITUATIONAL INTERVIEWS

In most interviewing processes, there is little structure to how questions are asked or rated. When all applicants are asked the same questions, the questions are often unrelated to the job. When the questions are job-related, interviewers frequently cannot agree on what constitutes a good versus poor response. And when they can agree, the socially desirable answer is often transparent to the interviewees. The result is an ineffective selection process.

Situational interviews are based on the premise that intentions predict behavior. Interview questions, derived from a job analysis, are turned into dilemmas. These dilemmas are then presented to applicants and their response elicited: "What would you do in this situation?" The dilemma makes it difficult for the applicant to answer the question with a socially desirable response. J.P. Morgan, General Electric, and McKinsey believe that with increased shareholder scrutiny, intense competition for talent, and the costs of hiring the wrong person, situational interviews are much more predictive (54 percent accuracy versus 7 percent accuracy) than traditional interviews. As a result, these companies and a growing number of other companies require all candidates to undergo a situational interview.

Situational interviews are usually administered by a panel where one person reads the questions and all the raters record and evaluate the answers. After each question is answered, the interviewers score the answer using a scoring guide. Scoring guides developed in advance by decision makers are designed to reflect the job requirements and the values of the organization. Hiring decisions are based on the sum of the scores. The result is an effective selection process that minimizes interviewer biases.

3.1.7 CONSIDER HIGH-PERFORMANCE PERSONALITY TRAITS IN HIRING PRACTICES

Five key personality traits can be used to describe personality in terms of predicting future job performance. These traits are called the "Big Five" dimensions:

1. Conscientiousness—the extent to which individuals are hardworking, organized, dependable, and persevering.
2. Extroversion—the degree to which individuals are gregarious, assertive, and sociable.
3. Agreeableness—the extent to which individuals are cooperative and warm.
4. Emotional stability—the degree to which individuals are secure, enthusiastic, and sensitive to others.
5. Openness to experience—the extent to which individuals are creative, curious, and cultured.

When these traits fit well with job requirements, job performance is optimal. For example, conscientious people perform well in all job categories except highly creative jobs (e.g., artist); people who rate high in extroversion and agreeableness perform well in sales; and people who rate high in extroversion, agreeableness, and emotional stability perform well as leaders. Mappings of personality traits to job category are readily available.

Personality assessments contribute unique information about future job performance—beyond information provided by, for example, general mental ability. Consider using such assessments in hiring practices, especially when jobs require significant levels of interpersonal or social interaction. Favor candidates whose personality traits fit well with the job requirements.

Acquisition

3.1.7

3.1.8 INFORM JOB APPLICANTS OF REFERENCE CHECKS

Interviewers should explicitly inform job applicants that their references will be checked to verify their characteristics, experiences, and work style. The applicant should be asked whom their references are and what he or she thinks they will say. If the applicant avoids or sidesteps these questions, the interviewer should take special note. The applicant's reaction to these questions often provides useful information as to where and how additional research should be focused.

Additionally, potential legal liability is associated with not contacting an applicant's references. Increasingly the courts are finding organizations liable for hiring dishonest, violent, or dangerous job applicants because the organizations failed to conduct reference checks. Likewise, organizations that refused a request for information are also being held liable. Given the legal exposure, a policy of documented, open disclosure to the applicant about the intention to check references is a prudent step in building an affirmative defense against future litigation.

Contact applicant references. Inform applicants that you will be contacting their references. This will elicit telling reactions from the applicants, provide information that can be corroborated or falsified by the references, and minimize legal liability for the organization.

3.1.9 FOCUS ON CULTURAL FIT AND VALUE CONGRUENCE

Cultural fit (i.e., employees share work style) and value congruence (i.e., employees share organizational values) positively impact employee attitudes and reduce the likelihood of employee attrition. Therefore, these factors should be a primary consideration in organizational hiring practices.

Although there is strong evidence that general mental ability (i.e., IQ) is the best general indicator of individual employee performance, the degree of cultural fit and value congruence is the best general indicator of group performance. Additionally, a highly intelligent employee who does not share organizational values or work well within a culture can compromise the performance of everyone around him or her—the high performance of one employee is more than offset by the reduced performance of many employees.

Therefore, when screening applicants, employers should focus on attributes that are difficult to change through training. For example, knowledge and skills for many positions can be effectively taught, whereas personality traits cannot.

Acquisition

3.1.9

3.2.1 TREAT EMPLOYEES AS ASSETS OF THE ORGANIZATION, NOT COSTS

Investing in employees is not altruism. It is smart business that yields long-term dividends.

Too many managers think of employees as expenses to the organization—compensation, fringe benefits, parking facilities, training, sick days, etc. Thinking of employees as expenses leads to treating employees as expenses. Employees who are treated as expenses act like expenses. They perform at the level necessary to avoid termination, not at the level necessary to achieve success; they view their job as a commodity and spend time and energy exploring alternative career paths; they do not take risks or make sacrifices for the company. A culture based on this type of thinking and acting is inconsistent with long-term success.

Employees are assets that appreciate with time—if they receive the proper level of investment. Managers who treat employees as vital human assets have more productive, satisfied, and committed workers. Companies that actively invest in their employees enjoy the long-term benefits associated with increased retention, the accrual of organizational knowledge, and an increased ability to recruit top talent.

Retention

3.2.1

3.2.2 HOLD MANAGERS ACCOUNTABLE FOR EMPLOYEE RETENTION

It is far less costly to retain employees than replace them. Direct costs of attrition include exit interviews, administrative activities, temporary workers, overtime, and replacement (planning, advertising, interviewing, and selection). Indirect costs include loss of knowledge, experience, and client relationships and negative impact on morale. Additionally, there is risk that new hires, after being trained, will not fit the job and organizational culture, leading to additional replacement efforts.

Given these considerable costs, managers should be held accountable for keeping the primary variables that contribute to the loss of employees:

- Low job satisfaction
- Low morale
- High stress
- Lack of support (e.g., training)
- Poor career development
- Lack of fairness and respect

Many causes of turnover are outside the control of managers. However, formally holding managers accountable for the causes that can be controlled will minimize attrition and clearly communicate to employees their importance to the organization. Track resignation rates by manager. Track the variables that contribute to resignations. Hold managers accountable for these variables—before the loss of talent and organizational assets becomes a problem.

3.2.3 ENSURE THAT EMPLOYEES UNDERSTAND THEIR BENEFITS

Retention

3.2.3

Benefits packages are important to both job seekers and present employees. Benefits include any form of compensation that isn't part of an employee's basic pay (e.g., stock options, 401(k) plan, health care, and maternity leave). Unfortunately, the complexity of such benefits makes them difficult to understand and use—resulting in many employees not appreciating the true value of their benefits package. For example, it is estimated that only two out of five employees believe their benefits compare favorably with other organizations. Such beliefs contribute to low morale and increased turnover.

Good communication and training regarding benefits is essential in retaining top talent. It takes time and effort to learn about health insurance, stock options, dental insurance, sick leave policies, and all of the other benefits to which employees are entitled. However, investing the necessary time and energy is a visible commitment to employees that the organization is interested in their welfare.

Support employees in understanding and taking full advantage of their benefits. If you can't promptly and confidently answer a benefit question, refer the employee to the appropriate person. Make basic information about benefits readily available to employees (e.g., brochures, Internet or Intranet sites, and videos). Consider bringing benefits representatives in for one-on-one employee training and counseling. Do not make the mistake of not informing employees, putting employees off, or delegating the responsibility of getting an answer to an employee.

3.2.4 CONDUCT EXIT INTERVIEWS WHEN EMPLOYEES RESIGN

Exit interviews are interviews conducted by an organization prior to an employee leaving. An exit interview has three goals: determine the reasons an employee has decided to leave the company; identify any systemic problems of the organization related to employee treatment or development; and end the employer-employee relationship on a positive, constructive note. Exit interviews can be conducted when employees leave voluntarily (e.g., resign or retire) or leave involuntarily (e.g., are terminated for cause or are downsized).

Studies consistently show that employees often provide inaccurate or incomplete feedback in exit interviews. When employees leave voluntarily, they tend not to share honest negative feedback for fear it will offend management. Offending management may hurt their chances of a positive reference or future employment with the organization should they want to return. When employees leave involuntarily, they are often inclined to retaliate by fabricating or exaggerating negative feedback. Therefore, exit interviews for employees who leave voluntarily are recommended when special measures are taken to attain valid feedback. Exit interviews for employees who are forced to leave are not recommended.

Conduct exit interviews when employees leave voluntarily, especially when the employees are considered "high performers" in the organization. The person conducting the exit interview should come from a neutral department (e.g., human resources). Since this is often a difficult emotional time for the employee, the interview should be structured to help both parties get through the interview in a positive, constructive manner. If an employee is unable or unwilling to participate in an exit interview or is uncomfortable doing so, offer the option of an exit survey. Exit surveys can be sent by mail some months after the employee leaves, and they often provide more objective feedback than an interview. When employees are forced to leave, a final meeting to discuss matters such as health benefits, job assistance, and counseling should be conducted—the parting should be as constructive and amicable as possible.

Retention

3.2.4

3.2.5 HONOR THE PAST

Honoring the past can be a powerful resource of inspiration, support, and knowledge for employees. The history of an organization provides real and relevant lessons, both good and bad, of organizational practice. Rather than ignoring or being disrespectful of the past, it is more beneficial to openly and constructively discuss the problems, solutions, successes, and failures that helped shape the culture and systems of the organization.

Use the lessons of the past to help shape the future. Do not challenge the pride and accomplishments of past eras. Rather, use events and principles from the organization's history as a bridge to help employees understand change and embrace new goals. Much like a person's family genealogy or cultural heritage, preserving and respecting the past of an organization is fundamental to understanding why things are the way they are. Honoring the past establishes a tradition of positive and constructive analysis of the organization and provides benchmarks against which future performance can be fairly and properly evaluated.

Retention

3.2.5

3.2.6 USE THE PAST AS A SOURCE FOR INSPIRATION AND INSTRUCTION

Instead of considering the past as dead history, managers should use it to inspire current work. The people, events, and changes in an organization represent an important heritage. Managers should educate current employees about the origin of the organization, its founders, and key events and eras in its history (e.g., major changes, changes in leadership, and new products). Knowledge of historical events creates an appreciation of the past, an understanding of the present, and a foundation upon which to think about the future.

Linking the past to the present allows managers to explain how and why things are done in the firm. It forms the identity of the organization. It provides a grounding of who did what to make significant events happen. Stories about heroes, founders, and employees who did something extraordinary create internal benchmarks against which people and actions can be evaluated. Stories about challenging eras, failed leaders, and unsuccessful products provide important organizational lessons to be avoided in the future.

The past helps employees understand where the organization has been—and where it is going. Learn from it. Use it.

Retention

3.2.6

3.2.7 CREATE ENVIRONMENTS WHERE EMPLOYMENT SECURITY IS ASSURED

Retention

3.2.7

Employment security is fundamental to organizational performance and prerequisite to the successful implementation of virtually all other management practices. Employee support, cooperation, and innovation cannot be sustained if employees believe that they will ultimately work themselves or their colleagues out of a job or if they believe that their employers view them as expendable assets.

Therefore, organizations should strive to create an environment in which employment security is assured and employees have the stability necessary to actively and enthusiastically work to achieve organizational goals. In organizations with a poor history or reputation of employment security, creating such an environment may require extreme actions; for example, employee agreements with guaranteed terms of employment. In less extreme circumstances, all that may be required is a stated policy supporting employment security followed by actions that prove the words. For example, Hypertherm, Inc., a metalworking firm operating in 60 countries, has had a policy for over 35 years of "no layoff" at any level. Management states that the "no layoff" policy isn't intended to be philanthropic. It is good business and allows every employee to concentrate on the firm's mission and customers.

An additional benefit of employment security is the increased requirement for management planning and discipline. When layoffs are a consideration of last resort, organizations must weigh new hiring and spending decisions more carefully. This results in leaner, more strategically sound organizations that are less likely to overreact to the highs and lows of economic and business cycles.

3.2.8 CREATE AN ENVIRONMENT THAT IS WORK/LIFE FRIENDLY

An increasing number of organizations have found that it makes good business sense to sponsor work/life programs. These organizations have identified gains such as the ability to attract and retain talent, reduced turnover, lower recruitment and training costs, increased productivity, and improved morale.

The most attractive work/life program features include:

- Flexible work options, such as flextime, job sharing, permanent part-time, flex-place, and/or a compressed work week.
- Leave benefits, such as maternity leave, family care leave, and emergency leave.
- Support services, such as medical and insurance coverage, elder care subsidies, child care centers, health and wellness programs, and scholarship assistance for children.

Consider work/life programs as a means of attracting and retaining talent and nurturing a happier, more stable, and more productive workforce. An organization not financially able to institute formal programs should still consider aspects of the programs that are inexpensive to implement and that have high value to employees (e.g., flextime).

Retention

3.2.8

3.2.9 TREAT EMPLOYEES THE SAME

Retention

3.2.9

A major risk of serving as a manager is being sued. Since the mid-1980s, the number of employee lawsuits has doubled every year. The costs are enormous, with the average jury verdict in wrongful termination cases averaging over $750,000. Organizations lose over 60 percent of the wrongful termination cases that go to jury.

Discrimination on the basis of sex, race, age, job tenure, or other classifications is both unacceptable and preventable. Obviously, managers should make conscious attempts to avoid such discrimination. However, proving that a manager did not engage in discriminatory behaviors is another matter. The easiest way for managers to prove that they treated employees fairly is to show they treated everyone the same. Managers must display a consistent pattern of interactions with employees. The courts take the concept of consistency seriously. For example, when employees are terminated for disciplinary reasons but claim wrongful termination based on discrimination, the courts look to whether other employees engaging in similar behaviors were terminated. If disciplinary treatment has been inconsistently applied, the verdicts tend to favor the plaintiffs.

Treat people in a consistent manner. Maintain documentation regarding hiring, promotion, termination, recognition and rewards, and disciplinary actions. Ensure that employee records are consistent with managerial actions. Provide written warning to employees for serious misconduct. Involve in performance appraisals all managers who work with an employee. If these managers are unaware of performance problems, they could later testify that an employee was a good performer, implying unfair treatment.

3.2.10 SEEK WAYS TO MINIMIZE STRESS

The American Stress Institute places the cost of stress into the $200 to $300 billion dollar range annually. Stress manifests itself in terms of compensation claims, medical costs, absenteeism, interpersonal conflict, litigation, workplace violence, higher health care costs, turnover, and inefficient business operations. The best defense against the financial and human costs of stress is proactive prevention and treatment.

Managers can use a number of strategies to help employees learn about and cope with negative stress at work. These strategies include such programs as meditation, social support, job redesign, flexible work schedules, telecommuting, and community outreach. In extreme cases, managers should consider retaining professional counseling support.

Each individual and situation is different. Managerial support and help must be flexible enough to fit the person. Listen, observe, and interact with employees to gain insight into the correct strategy. Remain vigilant to symptoms of stress in the organization—e.g., emotional outbursts, increased absenteeism and attrition, and nominal participation and volunteerism. Ignore the costs of stress at the organization's peril.

Retention

3.2.10

3.2.11 DEVELOP SYSTEMS THAT ENSURE ORGANIZATIONAL FAIRNESS AND JUSTICE

Employee perceptions of organizational justice are related to a number of work-related behaviors, including performance, absenteeism, volunteerism, morale, and employee retention. In short, when people perceive a lack of fairness in the organization, these variables suffer.

There are three basic types of organizational justice: (1) procedural justice, which refers to fair formal decision making procedures; (2) distributive justice, which refers to fair decision outcomes; and (3) interactional justice, which refers to fair interpersonal treatment by managers. Procedural justice has the greatest effect on employee commitment. It is the foundation for trust in management and a significant factor in employee attrition. Distributive justice has the greatest influence on general employee satisfaction. Interactional justice is a significant factor in both employee motivation and morale. Organizational justice is closely tied to employment security and is, therefore, prerequisite to the success of all other management systems.

Promote organizational justice through open two-way communication. Share information about how resources and rewards are allocated. Publish internal procedures and follow them in a consistent manner. Install comprehensive grievance procedures to enable employees to appeal issues to higher levels of management. Minimize unilateral decision making on matters that involve employment status and employee welfare and on processes that result in employee rewards or punishment.

Retention

3.2.11

3.2.12 DEAL WITH MORALE PROBLEMS

Avoiding or ignoring the emotional aspects of an organization is ill advised. Negative emotion impacts productivity and people's willingness to achieve company objectives. Happy workers are more loyal, more willing, and more giving than unhappy workers. Linked to physical well-being, positive emotions also reduce the direct and indirect costs associated with illness.

Anger, hostility, resentment, and anxiety contribute to personal and interpersonal dysfunction. Perceptions of being "wronged," lack of personal control over one's destiny, and feelings of being disconnected (not needed) lower morale.

Promote morale in the organization by:

- Engaging the workforce in "wellness" through diet, exercise, and education.
- Giving individuals and teams the accountability and resources needed to be successful.
- Linking employees to one another through common interests, personal missions, or other values.
- Providing opportunities to give back to the community and to each other in terms of time, expertise, teaching, or other forms of giving.
- Engaging qualified coaches to address productivity problems that are linked to emotional issues.
- Meeting basic employee needs (i.e., physical aspects of the workplace, benefits, and compensation).

These examples demonstrate practical ways to enhance the well-being of employees, which will enhance the well-being of the organization.

3.2.13 DO NOT AVOID OR SUPPRESS CONFLICT—MANAGE IT OPENLY

Retention

3.2.13

Many managers assume that conflict is negative. Consequently, they avoid it. This results in employees with unresolved issues and a sense of pessimism that those issues will be addressed.

Managers should deal with conflict openly and constructively. Conflict should be managed, not avoided. Conflict has been shown to help organizations stay in touch with their customers and to help leaders stay in touch with their employees. Open, constructive conflict stimulates motivation to deal with issues and provides a medium through which problems are aired, solutions are developed, and relationships are reaffirmed. Through open conflict, agreement, unity, and justice are often reached. Properly managed, conflict is not the problem—it is part of the solution.

The way in which people approach and deal with conflict determines its usefulness. Manage conflict in a way that benefits all parties by developing integrated, high-quality solutions. The protagonists' confidence is strengthened when they can constructively work through differences and still maintain a positive professional relationship. By contrast, managing conflict by ignoring it or by declaring a winner/loser results in escalated negotiation and/or one-sided imposed resolutions that fragment relationships.

Manage conflict openly and constructively and maintain emotional control. Strive for consensus on the issues when time permits. Use a mediator or mutually agreed upon decision maker when time is short.

3.2.14 BUILD TRUST IN ORGANIZATIONS

Organizations in which employees trust management enjoy many benefits, including improved cooperation, communication, morale, retention, and productivity. Such trust is not simply or quickly invoked. It must be built up in the organization over time by establishing a history of honest and open communication, fair treatment and social justice, and words backed by actions.

Strategies to build trust in organizations include these:

- Be respectful of employees in public and private.
- Meet deadlines or time commitments made to employees.
- Treat employees in a consistent manner.
- Express and share values and goals. Spend time discussing common interests, needs, and plans.
- Allow employees to externalize their feelings in a constructive manner.
- Do not betray employees by gossiping or talking badly about them to others.
- Use punishment for serious transgressions only and after all other alternatives have been exhausted.
- Err on the side of being overly fair.

Retention

3.2.15

3.2.15 CONSIDER LAYOFFS AS A COST-REDUCTION METHOD OF LAST RESORT

Despite its cyclic popularity, the use of layoffs as a means of cost reduction does not yield long-term benefits that are significantly different from benefits gained by firms that achieve cost reductions in other ways. Additionally, layoffs cost organizations in the form of reduced employee motivation, interruption of operational flow, and loss of organizational knowledge.

This is not to suggest that layoffs should never occur. For example, layoffs may be necessary when restructuring an organization, when merging with or acquiring another organization, or when addressing employee misconduct or poor performance. Do not use layoffs, however, as a means of addressing short-term goals at the neglect of longer-term problems. The point is nicely summarized by a Federal Express executive:

> *No-layoff is a commitment, not a policy. There are no guarantees, but the firm is on record as having a strong commitment to make every effort not to lay off personnel except in the most extreme economic circumstances, as determined by the chief executive officer.*

In cases where layoffs are necessary, make sure the process of determining who is to be laid off is clearly communicated to employees and then is fairly implemented. Common alternatives to layoffs include delaying nice-to-have upgrades to infrastructure and equipment, suspending the implementation of new business lines, delaying new hire start dates, revoking job offers, freezing salaries and promotions, requesting volunteers for unpaid vacations, and requesting voluntary retirement for senior staff.

3.2.16 FAVOR MARKET-BASED COMPENSATION FOR BASE SALARIES

Linking financial incentives to behaviors or goals does not lead to sustained improvements in the performance of complex cognitive tasks, although it may lead to improvements in the performance of simple physical tasks. Even in the latter case, however, the costs are high and often outweigh the benefits:

- Employees tend to focus on how well tasks are performed, rather than on the best way to perform tasks; quality suffers for output.
- Employees develop a dysfunctional preoccupation with extrinsic rewards that discourages risk taking, creativity, and innovation.
- Intrinsic motivation of employees is undermined in most circumstances, though the effect is less dramatic for tasks that are interesting.
- Risk of compensation-related litigation increases as a result of accuracy, fairness, and bias issues associated with performance measurement.

Market-based compensation systems, by contrast, focus on attracting and retaining talent, rather than attempting to manipulate performance. Such systems avoid the problems of incentive-based approaches by setting salaries based on regional market averages for specific jobs.

Favor market-based compensation systems over performance-based or tenure-based compensation systems. Set base salaries at levels slightly higher than average to ensure competitive compensation. Consider additional financial and nonfinancial incentives to augment base salaries, but implement such programs with caution.

3.3.1 USE PERFORMANCE APPRAISALS FOR EMPLOYEE DEVELOPMENT ONLY

Performance appraisals are typically used for multiple functions, including awarding pay increases, setting goals, making promotion choices, counseling, coaching, and mentoring. This is commonly considered a good practice—when formally meeting with an employee only once or twice a year, it is efficient to cover as many things as possible.

However, this bundling of functions is a key reason why appraisals are disliked and ineffective. For example, most organizations use performance appraisals to determine promotions and pay increases. This linkage focuses all appraisal-related discussions between managers and employees on promotion and pay, rather than on constructive dialogue about employee development. Managers are biased to provide soft reviews. They usually do not want to deny employees pay increases or promotions, and they generally seek to avoid the confrontations that often come with critical reviews. Employees, by contrast, are distracted from the substance of the appraisal. They are preoccupied with the financial implications of critical feedback and, as a result, are more defensive than reflective about their past performance and future development. The point of the appraisal is lost. The outcome often stifles motivation as well as undermines the very corrective actions the appraisal seeks to bring about.

To avoid the problems associated with the use of performance appraisals for numerous functions, employ them for development purposes only. The single focus results in more productive manager-employee discussion, plans, and follow-up.

Development

3.3.1

3.3.2 MEET WITH EMPLOYEES ON A REGULAR BASIS TO DISCUSS PERFORMANCE

Managers should conduct periodic meetings with employees to discuss employees' performance. The meetings should be brief, informal, and participative. The objective of these meetings is to identify performance problems in a timely manner, discuss ways to resolve performance problems, and help employees to be successful.

A failure to conduct meetings of this type can result in a number of problems:

- Minor performance problems can become major, costly issues.
- Problems and concerns are forgotten—or it becomes too late to address them.
- It becomes difficult to assess an employee's ability to meet performance expectations.
- Employees believe managers are not interested in their progress, problems, or situation.

These meetings should be brief—no longer than 30 minutes. They should be supportive, developmental in tone, and nonjudgmental. Each employee should be encouraged to be a full participant. By dominating the conversation, the manager detracts from his or her ability to gain the employee's interest or respect. It is important not to discuss promotion, merit pay, or performance evaluation. These topics are for another meeting at another time.

Development

3.3.2

Development

3.3.3

3.3.3 CULTIVATE CREATIVITY, RISK TAKING, AND CONTRARIAN THINKING

Creative people see events, people, and things in unique ways. They make unusual connections that others miss. Risk takers seize opportunities and explore uncharted territories. Contrarians challenge conventional assumptions and popular beliefs. They ensure that decisions are sound and well directed. Combined, these qualities produce a culture in which new and better ways to achieve goals are the norm.

Properly nurtured, these qualities reproduce. Therefore, it is critical to promote these qualities actively in an organization. Strategies include the following:

- Encourage experimentation. Install controls to minimize the cost of failure.
- Do not punish failure. Learn from it.
- Tolerate difference. Diversity promotes creativity.
- Celebrate examples of creativity—inside and outside the organization.
- Encourage the "why." If people don't know why something is, make it safe for them to reveal that fact and get answers.
- Avoid policies and behaviors that inhibit creativity—e.g., homogenous work environments, restrictive dress codes, and ridiculing of new ideas.

Organizations that embrace contrarian thinking, risk taking, and creativity remain healthy and innovative over time. They continue to grow and replenish. They consistently outperform their competitors. Organizations without these qualities soon stagnate.

3.3.4 IMPLEMENT A VOLUNTEER-ONLY MENTOR PROGRAM

A mentor is an experienced, productive senior employee who helps in the development of a less experienced employee (a protégé). Mentors provide personal, professional, and psychological support for protégés, which reduces the time required for employees to meaningfully contribute to and integrate with the culture.

Mentors also act as "culture carriers" in that they teach protégés how to behave, how to relate to others, and what traditions and rituals to follow. Mentors provide a confidential sounding board for employees dealing with actual or perceived problems.

The most successful mentor/protégé programs are voluntary and are allowed to end any time the mentor or protégé chooses, without fear of punishment. Nonvoluntary mentor programs often create resentment and frustration among mentors. These mentors pass on (intentionally or unintentionally) their negative feelings to protégés. Not only do such nonvoluntary programs typically fail, they incur the additional risk of multiplying negativity and low morale throughout the organization.

Implement volunteer-only mentor programs. Set clear expectations that are agreed upon by participants. Successful mentors should be experienced and well regarded in the organization. Consider training for first-time mentors, offering incentives to develop themselves and their protégés. Successful protégés should be emotionally stable, flexible, and eager to achieve. Screen protégé candidates for these qualities in advance.

Development

3.3.4

3.3.5 IMPLEMENT CAREER DEVELOPMENT PROGRAMS

Development

3.3.5

Doctors attend seminars, workshops, and conferences to update their knowledge, skills, and credentials. Engineers and CPAs must continue formal training to maintain their certification status. Lawyers continually update themselves on new law, trends, and precedents.

Too many managers fail to do the same. Research indicates that superior management occurs in organizations that require a mix of continuous formal (e.g., workshops) and informal (e.g., reading) learning. Therefore, managers should read books, take courses, attend workshops, learn from other managers, and invest time and energy into keeping their skills sharp and up to date.

There are things managers do not know about or do not have the skill to implement. Investing in knowledge, skill, and competency improvement is the way to keep up with the science and art of management. As doctors, CPAs, engineers, teachers, and lawyers have demonstrated, continuous learning is key to professional excellence.

3.3.6 USE MULTISOURCE FEEDBACK TO EVALUATE PERFORMANCE

Multisource feedback—commonly referred to as 360-degree feedback—involves gathering information about a person from multiple sources and then using the sum of the information from these sources to perform employee evaluations. Sources of feedback commonly include direct reports, peers, supervisors, and customers.

The rationale behind multisource feedback is sound. Different people in an organization have different opportunities to observe a person's behavior. Considering feedback from these sources provides a more comprehensive and accurate view of an employee's overall performance. Additionally, multisource feedback is perceived to be more objective and credible than feedback from a single source (e.g., feedback from the manager only). This increases the chances that the feedback will be received constructively and will effect positive change.

Evidence supporting the benefits of multisource feedback at the individual level is strong. Feedback is more accurate, credible, and less prone to individual biases (e.g., gender and ethnic). Evidence supporting an organizational benefit is mostly anecdotal or assumed—there is currently little empirical evidence supporting an overall effect on organizational performance. A likely reason is the social dynamics that generally result from appraisals: they often become popularity contests, resulting in increased political maneuvering by employees. The productivity and morale costs of this social dynamic may cancel any positive effects realized at the individual level.

Use multisource feedback when evaluating employee performance, but do so with caution. The feedback is most effective when delivered in a relevant context—e.g., at the end of a project. It is least effective when delivered at an arbitrary interval—e.g., at an annual or semiannual review. Use a systematic method to select the sources. For example, use a randomly selected subset of the total feedback collected. Do not let the person being evaluated select the sources. Keep sources confidential.

Development

3.3.6

Development

3.3.7

3.3.7 AVOID SIMILAR-TO-ME BIAS

There is a tendency for people to favor others like themselves. This tendency is referred to as the similar-to-me bias. Left unchecked, it can undermine the quality and fairness of decisions regarding hiring, promotions, pay increases, and job assignments. Typically, this bias is not the result of conscious decision processes and is in fact found in organizations across cultures.

Research indicates that managers generally rate employees who share a similar race, age, education, religion, family structure, or political affiliations more highly than employees of lesser similarity. The bias is more pronounced in volatile or complex environments, likely because of the perceived need for increased communication and interaction. In any event, it is important to guard against similar-to-me bias for practical, ethical, and legal reasons. First, it does not serve the performance interests of an organization to favor similarity over merit. Second, it is unethical treatment of employees to permit such practices. Third, in certain circumstances, there are legal consequences for not actively guarding against the bias.

Actively guarding against the similar-to-me bias increases the perception of social equity and justice in the organization and advances organizational performance through promotion based on merit. Awareness of the bias is the first step toward prevention. Additionally, use multisource feedback (i.e., feedback from peers and customers) to minimize the bias and increase the accuracy and fairness of evaluative decisions.

3.3.8 FAVOR DEVELOPING STRENGTHS OVER CORRECTING WEAKNESSES

Managers should not assume that employee weaknesses must be corrected. Spending time, energy, and resources to change people to remediate such weakness is a costly affair that provides nominal benefits to the organization. Helping employees to develop their talents, by contrast, is an effective strategy to help organizations become more competitive.

The reason for favoring developing strengths is that people are hard to change. The time and energy required to fix weaknesses (e.g., improving a person's interpersonal skills and helping a person think more strategically) is enormous. A survey of more than 80,000 managers from over 400 companies indicated that successful managers focused their efforts more on maximizing the strengths of employees than trying to alter deficits. This survey finding is corroborated by research in the learning sciences. For example, research in neuroscience indicates that people learn, improve, and change more dramatically in those areas of the brain that have the strongest synaptic connections—i.e., it is easier to build on existing wiring in the brain than to build new wiring.

It is neither realistic nor preferable for managers to ignore weaknesses. Managers should expect employees to develop some of their weaknesses. This should, however, be considered the exception and not the rule. Favor developing the strengths of employees over correcting their weaknesses. Managing around employee deficits is usually less expensive than remedying them. This results in a greater payoff for employees in terms of enjoyment and promotion and for the organization in terms of reduced costs and increased productivity.

Development

3.3.8

3.3.9 CREATE A CULTURE THAT IS RECEPTIVE TO CONTINUOUS CHANGE

Cultures quickly harden. This occurs because people generally prefer stability. Stable organizational environments, however, are extinct. Consequently, management must build resilience into their organizations—the inherent capability to learn, adapt, and execute. For example, Toyota uses a very deliberate, continuous change approach to improve the efficiency of its production processes. Over the years, the ongoing change has become a part of employees' expectations and Toyota's organizational culture.

Managers can best achieve such resilience by developing organizations that exist in "liquid states"—i.e., ready and receptive to change. The liquid state is not natural for organizations. It must be actively nurtured and maintained; otherwise, the organization becomes inflexible and resistant to change.

Liquid states are noticeable when employees ask "why" and "why not." Reinvention and irreverence are viewed as cunning and necessary organizational characteristics. Diversity is more than tolerated—it is encouraged. Liquid states are the product of cultural norms that are dissatisfied with the status quo, encourage creativity and risk taking, and continuously and critically evaluate the underlying assumptions behind decisions.

Organizational cultures tend to harden with time. Don't let them. Keep the organizational culture fluid and dynamic—potent. Hard, inflexible cultures kill organizations. Promote contrarian thinking. Invite dialogue and feedback on decisions. Recognize and reward instances of creativity and prudent risk taking in the organization.

3.3.10 EMPOWER EMPLOYEES WITH AUTHORITY AND ACCOUNTABILITY

"Empowerment" is ineffective when it is not accompanied by authority and accountability. Employees with the skills necessary to achieve specific goals should be given the authority to do so—and then held accountable for achieving them. Empowerment without authority and accountability leads to feeble execution and frustration in the best of circumstances and unethical or criminal behavior in the worst of circumstances. In both extremes, it leads to failure.

Do not hold employees accountable for achieving goals without giving them the authority to do so. Conversely, do not give managers or employees authority to execute without holding them accountable for achieving specific goals. Accountability without authority is unjust. Authority without accountability is dangerous. Give employees the authority they need to accomplish goals. Hold them accountable for achieving those goals.

3.3.11 EMPHASIZE "LEARNING FROM EXPERIENCE" TO DEVELOP LEADERSHIP

The ability to "learn from experience" is the ability to derive new knowledge and skills from real-world experiences and quickly change attitudes and behaviors based on real-world experiences. This ability is surprisingly unique. It does not correlate with common measures of learning or intelligence, such as IQ or grades, yet it is among the most powerful predictors of future leadership performance.

Successful leaders learn from experience effectively and have a rich history of challenging experiences—including failures and defining moments. Unsuccessful leaders, by contrast, lack this ability or history or both. Therefore, it is important to emphasize challenging real-world experiences in leadership development programs. Two characteristics of effective learning experiences come up consistently in research: (1) challenging situations with problems to solve and choices to make under conditions of risk and (2) supportive environments with supervisors and mentors who provide positive role models and constructive support. Such experiences help people develop self-confidence and self-awareness, key competencies that distinguish average performers from star performers.

Leadership is a skill that can be learned—through rich real-world experiences. There is little evidence that proves that leadership skills can be effectively developed through classroom training or similar modalities. Assign tough jobs for top leadership candidates early in their career. This is important for learning and for employee retention. Failure is important to this process. Do not punish it. Emphasize the need to grow with each experience. Development is a demand pull—the demands of the job pull the person to develop new skills and not to rely solely on successful habits of the past.

3.4.1 PUT EMPLOYEES FIRST. SHAREHOLDER VALUE WILL FOLLOW

Shareholder value is best served by putting employees' interests foremost in the organization. Giving employees the security, resources, and incentives they need to be successful enables an organization to realize the potential of the workforce. Research indicates that organizations that put employees first (i.e., favor employee interests over the perceived interests of customers and shareholders) have higher sales, higher net income, and higher market value than organizations that put customers or shareholders before employees. In other words, putting employees first is equivalent to putting customers and shareholders first.

Putting employees first means:

- Ensuring employment security.
- Letting employees know they are "first" and then proving that fact through actions.
- Using self-managed teams in organization design. Peer-based control and team-member "buy in" lead to higher levels of accountability and initiative.
- Developing employee knowledge and skills through increased training and improved communication.
- Linking financial incentives to the achievement of specific organizational goals.
- Hiring selectively, making sure new hires are intelligent and share values common to the organization.
- Making layoffs the cost-reduction method of last resort.

Organizations that put employees first develop high-performance cultures. High-performance cultures make for happy customers. Happy customers make for happy shareholders. Put employees first. Shareholder value will follow.

3.4.2 AVOID INTERNAL COMPETITION. EMPHASIZE EXTERNAL COMPETITION

Using internal competition to try to improve performance is common in Western-style management. The rationale for the practice is usually based on a belief in the basic virtues of competition and analogies with coaching techniques in sports.

The fact is that internal competition reduces rather than promotes organizational performance, and analogies with sports are only valid for simple, repetitive tasks. Internal competition is generally counterproductive and should be avoided. Examples of internal competition include contests between divisions, units, or individuals; forced distribution systems in which evaluations and promotions are based on relative versus objective measures of performance; individual recognition and reward programs (e.g., employee of the month); and published rankings of performance measures.

Emphasizing external competition, however, tends to focus organizations on activities that are key to overall success. For example, Southwest Airlines found that internal competition and company infighting increased in the absence of a viable external competitor. This quickly changed, however, with the introduction of the United Shuttle service. Energy spent on internal competition and company infighting was quickly refocused on competing with United. The emphasis on an external adversary promoted internal communication, increased cooperation, and fostered a sense of unity that was necessary for optimal organizational performance.

3.4.3 CULTIVATE A STAKEHOLDER CULTURE

A stakeholder culture refers to a workforce that feels a deep personal responsibility to make an organization a success and believes that it has the ability and authority to do so. Organizations that successfully cultivate stakeholder cultures benefit from increased employee loyalty, altruism, and stewardship. The only potential liability associated with stakeholder cultures is their resistance to change. If handled improperly, change initiatives can threaten the sense of responsibility and authority employees have for the organization, leading employees to subvert change efforts so that the organization is not harmed.

Attributes of strong stakeholder cultures include:

- Control—Employees have significant control over relevant aspects of the organization.
- Knowledge—Employees have significant knowledge about a relevant aspect of the organization.
- Investment—Employees have invested significant levels of time and energy in a relevant aspect of the organization.

It is traditionally believed that ownership of stock or stock options positively contributes to positive stakeholder behavior in employees. Recent evidence shows that this is not the case, at least in times of market volatility or large swings in share prices. Therefore, cultivate a stakeholder culture by developing psychological ownership in employees (i.e., control, knowledge, and investment). These attributes are largely immune to fluctuations in share price. Delegate control and responsibility for important projects and tasks. Invest in training and career development. Allow employees sufficient time to achieve expertise in specialized areas of the organization. Use equity incentives with caution.

3.4.4 MINIMIZE STATUS DISTINCTIONS

For an organization to perform at peak levels, it must realize the potential of its people. This potential can only be realized when people are willing to invest time and energy and make a commitment to the organization—i.e., when they perceive that the organization is worthy of more than the minimal effort required to do their job. One strategy used by high-performance organizations to achieve this level of employee investment is to reduce status and power distinctions in the organization.

Two principle types of status and power distinctions should be minimized: symbolic and compensatory. Symbolic distinctions include differences in job titles, physical space, and dress. Compensatory distinctions include differences in wages, work/life flexibility, and eligibility for special bonus or reward programs.

Minimizing distinctions does not mean eliminating them. Clearly, market rates for different skills and experience dictate that people within an organization will be paid at different levels. Symbolic distinctions are often necessary to transact business efficiently. However, extreme disparities and unnecessary distinctions are counter-productive. For example, in 1995, then-CEO of Southwest Airlines, Herb Kelleher, agreed to freeze his base salary when the pilots agreed to freeze their base salaries. This gesture by Kelleher minimized the power distinctions between the CEO and the rest of the company. The gesture demonstrated a commitment to putting the company first and illustrated by example what "putting the company first" meant at the time—controlling costs.

Eliminate unnecessary status and power distinctions—meaningless job titles, "status by the foot" cubicle/office space, and exclusive reward programs that are available to only certain members of the organization. Minimize necessary status and power distinctions—set base salaries at or near market rates for jobs, assign titles and physical space by functional need, and apply policies consistently to everyone in the organization.

3.4.5 MAINTAIN A POSITIVE EMOTIONAL CLIMATE

The emotional climate of an organization refers to employees' perceptions of how they are treated in an organization—how they are treated by management and by other employees. Organizations with positive emotional climates have better customer service, lower turnover, and higher productivity than their less positive counterparts. A primary factor contributing to a positive emotional climate is the visible intention of management to make the climate positive through their words and actions. By contrast, attempting to improve the emotional climate using monetary rewards and opportunities for advancement has been found to be ineffectual.

Strategies to promote a positive emotional climate include these:

- Support employees with emotionally difficult jobs (e.g., nurses).
- Train employees in healthy emotional expression.
- Lead by example—be positive and constructive.
- Create opportunities for relationship building.
- Consider attitudes of people when assembling teams.
- Maintain emotional control in public and private.
- Remove "toxic employees" who spread negativity.

Maintain a positive emotional climate by visibly trying to maintain a positive emotional climate. To a large extent, such a climate is a self-fulfilling prophecy. Strictly enforce standards of conduct in the organization. Ensure that employees are treated in a respectful, positive manner. Inappropriate behavior (e.g., loss of emotional control, disrespectful treatment, and spreading rumors about people) and negativity are contagious, and they should not be allowed to take root in the organization.

3.4.6 SHARE THE REWARDS OF SUCCESS WITH ALL EMPLOYEES

Traditional compensation systems typically pay employees fixed salaries, with the promise of annually scheduled increases. These systems are generally ineffective because they fail to link the performance of individual employees with the performance of the organization. Additionally, such systems tend to reinforce the expectation of regular increases in salary regardless of the financial health of the organization. This fosters an entitlement culture, resulting in an irrational disconnect between employee and organizational reality.

Compensation systems that are at least in part contingent on organizational performance (e.g., gain sharing, profit sharing, and stock ownership) outperform traditional compensation systems in terms of positively affecting organizational performance. These systems foster a culture that understands the relationship between compensation and performance—i.e., when the organization is successful, compensation increases; when the organization is not successful, compensation decreases.

Effective compensation systems epitomize the proverb "a rising tide lifts all boats." Implement compensation systems that provide a clear cause-effect relationship between individual or group performance and the performance of the organization. For example, it would be meaningless to implement a profit sharing program in an organization with no near-term prospect of achieving profits. Significant variation in contingent compensation can hurt morale and negatively impact motivation. Favor simple schemes that promote the perception of equity and fairness in the organization.

3.4.7 LABEL DIFFERENT BUSINESS AND MANAGEMENT ERAS

Change is inevitable. An organization that does not embrace change will fail. Unfortunately, the cost of organization change is often its history. Organizations that forget their history lose their identities and sense of continuity of what they are about. This leads to confusion about the identity and mission of the organization and sacrifices a heritage and legacy in which employees can participate.

One way for organizations to both embrace change and avoid these difficulties is to label management eras. An example of era labeling can be found in a telecommunications firm that for years was engaged in teaching, implementing, and solidifying their goal-setting system. The employees referred to this time period as the "goal-setting and feedback era." A new CEO arrived and eliminated most of the goal-setting processes and systems. He downsized, was impersonal, and became embroiled in a number of expensive lawsuits. His tenure was referred to as the "hire, fire, and sue" era—not as positive as the goal-setting era, but part of the company's history nonetheless.

By labeling eras, the history and the identity of the organization becomes a part of storytelling and lore. This provides opportunities to talk about the firm, which creates a sense of oneness and helps with the socialization of incoming employees who are just learning about the value system and character of the organization. Label eras. Teach the history of the organization to employees. Without heritage and legacy, organizations are just another place to work. They are, in effect, commodities.

3.4.8 ENGAGE EMPLOYEES IN ORGANIZATION-SPONSORED COMMUNITY OUTREACH

One way to demonstrate good corporate citizenship and to improve morale is to encourage employees to participate in organization-sponsored community outreach programs. Employee involvement in the social, economic, and civic development of communities sends a message that the company is interested in more than market share, revenue generation, and profit margins.

Giving time and energy to these programs promotes goodwill from the community and generates a sense of satisfaction and community participation among employees. Management should, when possible, change schedules and provide company resources to support employee participation. Management should also consider matching funds when employees make financial contributions to community programs.

Supporting community outreach projects a positive image of the company. It makes attracting good job candidates easy. It helps retain employees. It improves the morale of the organization. And it helps the communities where employees and their families live.

Productivity

3.4.8

3.4.9 ACTIVELY PROMOTE TEAM SPIRIT IN GROUPS

Team spirit is the morale and confidence of a team. Members of teams with strong team spirit are willing to invest more time and energy on behalf of the team. They exhibit higher levels of cooperation, learning and helping behaviors, and creativity and productivity. Consequently, teams with strong team spirit consistently outperform teams with little or no team spirit.

Strategies to promote team spirit include these:

- Give teams a clear purpose. Make sure that members know the team mission and how it relates to the strategic success of the organization.
- Keep teams together. Clearly define the team membership and keep it as stable as possible.
- Ensure fairness. Install standards, policies, and procedures to ensure that team members are treated fairly and equitably.
- Use group rewards. Share recognition and rewards gained through team accomplishments equally among team members.
- Facilitate cooperation. Position team members near one another in open workspaces; they should be able to see and speak to one another easily.
- Build relationships. Structure fun nonwork-related activities during and outside of work.

Productivity

3.4.9

3.4.10 EMPHASIZE LISTENING IN DISCUSSIONS AND MEETINGS

Approximately 10 percent of a 40-hour workweek is wasted because of poor communication. Poor listening causes a majority of these communication problems. Therefore, it is important to emphasize listening in both one-on-one and group meetings and to provide training on effective listening skills whenever possible.

Demonstrate the importance of what people have to say by taking special measures to avoid interruptions (e.g., close doors and turn off cell phones). Look at the person or persons talking to you. Do not daydream, stare at a notepad, or play with your pen. Focus on the person. Avoid distracting body language (e.g., looking at your clock or watch). Rather than thinking about what you are going to say in response, focus instead on trying to understand what the person is saying and how the person is saying it. Learn to be comfortable with silence-—a pause is not an invitation to speak.

Listening to others requires patience, effort, and concentration. Good listeners ask meaningful questions and rephrase key points to make sure they are interpreting accurately what is being said. Improved listening not only improves overall productivity, but also creates feelings of goodwill by showing people that they are important enough to receive your undivided attention.

Productivity

3.4.10

3.4.11 DE-EMPHASIZE THE HIERARCHY OF THE ORGANIZATIONAL CHART

Organizational charts are used for a variety of purposes. Unfortunately, indicating the relative importance of people—intentionally or unintentionally—is often one of them.

Organizational charts are useful tools for understanding the design of an organization. They indicate the location of authority and accountability within an organization; the size of organizational units; and, in some cases, the lines of communication. Their utility comes largely from the use of a hierarchical representation, locating senior management at the top of the hierarchy and lower levels of management toward the bottom.

In most contexts, however, hierarchical representations are interpreted as an endorsement of autocratic or elitist management. They are perceived as promoting a form of classism in which people lower on the hierarchy are considered less important than people on the top. The hierarchical structure can become culturally self-fulfilling, leaning the organization toward a command-and-control style of management. This has a detrimental effect on morale, communication, and the overall flexibility of the organization.

Use the organizational chart as it was intended: for planning and organizing. Be selective about how and with whom the organizational chart is shared. Avoid posting the charts in public locations or on web sites. Do not circulate the charts widely as documents or e-mails. Consider alternative forms of representation other than a top-down hierarchy. Many organizations, for example, invert the hierarchy to make a statement to employees that management is there to support rather than oppress. Even when the management style of an organization is autocratic, it serves the performance interests of the organization to be subtle about the fact. De-emphasize the hierarchy of the organization to employees.

3.4.12 FOCUS ON FIXING PROBLEMS, NOT PUNISHING PEOPLE

Punishment is a powerful means of modifying behavior. However, it has serious side effects that generally outweigh the value of the behavior change.

In cases where employees engage in inappropriate acts or intentional negligence, punishment is appropriate. In all other cases, the use of punishment as a means of addressing a problem is generally counterproductive.

First and foremost, punishment encourages employees to avoid the punishment. This reduces the willingness of the culture to take risks and act on new ideas.

Second, punishment rarely addresses the underlying causes of problems, such as having insufficient resources or time to complete a task. Punishment in these circumstances lowers morale and reduces the perception of fair treatment within the organization.

Third, punishment is difficult to administer consistently and effectively. For punishment to be effective, a manager must be present at the work site so that an employee can be punished as soon as an infraction occurs. Employees who get away with unacceptable behaviors without being punished are essentially rewarded for beating the rules.

Finally, the results of punishment can be difficult to predict. Unintended consequences include employee attrition, revenge, sabotage, workplace violence, and avoidance of behaviors

The costs of punishment are high. The side effects are costly and difficult to predict. Fix problems when they occur. Reserve the use of punishment for circumstances in which an immediate and severe intervention is required.

Productivity

3.4.12

3.4.13 SHARE KEY FINANCIAL INFORMATION WITH EMPLOYEES

Open-book management is based on the practice of sharing vital performance and financial information with employees at all levels of the organization. Information sharing is motivational, and it cultivates loyalty and a sense of ownership among employees. Employees who have access to financial information become business-smart and are better able to respond quickly and intelligently to a changing environment.

The open-book approach is more a philosophy than a sequential step-by-step procedure. Every company has certain pivotal numbers and measures. Knowing the numbers allows everyone to understand and care about his or her role in the operation of the company. Opening the books in this way can have startling results. It has been shown to increase morale, productivity, market share, profits, and return on assets. These effects have been observed in organizations of all sizes and across industries.

Many managers resist the notion of sharing critical financial information with employees. The benefits of doing so, however, clearly outweigh the costs. Embrace open-book management principles. Publish vital company information on a regular basis in a visible manner (e.g., a bulletin board). Educate people in the organization about which data are important and why.

3.4.13

AFTERWORD

After over seventy-five years of research there is now a body of knowledge that managers can apply to their daily operations and strategic decision-making. The largely empirically-derived knowledge contained in this book has been transferred from journals, books, and archives without jeopardizing the rigor, methods, and caveats expressed by the researchers who have produced the results. Practicing managers have in the form of these guidelines job and work-related suggestions, principles, and concepts similar to what professionals in medicine, law, and engineering have in their respective areas of expertise.

Research has found that managers rarely read, let alone cite the findings offered by organizational scientists who typically have complex statistical models at the core of their reports. Managers tend to prefer concrete observations to abstract generalizations. The guidelines presented in this book are concrete generalizations influenced by empirical, scientific, and logical studies and analyses.

In the growth and evolution of a field such as management there eventually is a "moment of truth," a point at which those who are practicing ask "What is next, where do we go from here?" The question is asked because there is a desire by many in the field to achieve visible progress and acquire greater attention and respect for the work they perform. The value, impact, and stature of managerial work are enhanced when a field becomes stable and is held in high esteem by the public.

Lessons from Mature Professions

Generally it is agreed that management does not have a common body of accepted knowledge that a practitioner must possess. However, tracing and imitating some of the steps in the professional evolution of medicine, law, and engineering could benefit the practice of management. Managers can learn from the positive features and practices of these developed professions. These professions have matured and continue to exist because societies value their expert application of knowledge. A respected and mature profession is distinguished by core values that transcend the self-interest of their practitioners, offers a body of knowledge that is both applicable and useful, and practices according to high ethical and moral standards.

A review of the history of the professionalization of medicine, law, and engineering illustrates a pattern of evolution along these lines:

1. The development of a recognized, testable set of guidelines that offer practitioners value in solving problems, resolving controversies, or improving the efficiency of practice. This is referred to as a "common body of knowledge."
2. The guidelines become a part of the educational content/knowledge base for educating those aspiring to become a part of the profession.
3. The creation of an oversight body that offers governance, a code of conduct, and a code of ethics.
4. Increased acceptance of standards and guidelines about what practitioners should do in performing their roles and improving their contributions to clients, organizations, and society.
5. As a field evolves into a profession there is a point when practitioners have to prove or display their knowledge and skill. In most professions this validation involves a form of testing or certification.

In order for management to become a mature profession, leaders must point the way; participants who passionately advance professionalization, and individuals who attract others to become engaged in the work required to professionalize the practice of managing assets. These five steps have a higher likelihood of success if management as a field assembles a common body of knowledge. Can the Guidelines for Excellence® serve as a body of knowledge? This is a question that we offer for debate, consideration, and analysis. We would like to have managers begin the discussion, test the guidelines in action, and offer their own plan for becoming more professional in their behavior and thinking.

A Long Journey Ahead

Today management should not be referred to as a profession. Unlike physicians, lawyers, or engineers, managers do not obtain licenses to practice. Also, they do not swear to uphold a standard code of conduct to perform their roles. If management were a profession, practitioners would not be allowed to practice unless they were certified. Some critics of the professionalization of management believe that enforcing a "certification only" rule would be impossible to enforce.

Unfortunately, the recent public view of management has deteriorated because the primary measures of successful management are self-promotion and financial gain. The lack of professionalism among some managers is associated with unethical and criminal practices and greed, which continue to find their way into the news.

The five steps taken by the most respected professions would seem to be benchmarks to initiate the public discussion and debate about the practice of management. Currently, practitioners are a loose confederation of individuals who are positioned throughout organizations and possess a wide range of education and experience. In most cases practitioners do not have access to the type of guidelines found in this book. Instead most managers use intuition, observation, and the knowledge they have acquired over time to make decisions. A knowledgeable management population would be aware of how guidelines emerge, where they fit, when they must be modified, and when they should be ignored.

The guidelines in this book are offered as an attempt to improve the growth, development, and increased sophistication of management. Perhaps, at some point in the future management will evolve from a field of study, considered only as an "art", to a more professional endeavor that uses empirical evidence and a common body of knowledge to improve its value and impact on organizational effectiveness.

Adopting the status quo and accepting the premise that managing assets is only an "art" is not what this book is about. This book offers guidance on how to achieve improved individual, team, and organizational effectiveness by using a more balanced science-art approach. Our hope is that after reading this book, you believe that it is possible to implement many of the guidelines. These guidelines offer tools to revitalize the practice of management in terms of public confidence, as well as to motivate managers to weigh carefully the benefits and costs of becoming more professional.

Guidelines as a Starting Point

The professionalization of management is and will remain a controversial subject. The strongest, most influential professions have bodies of knowledge and groups of people who are intellectually cohesive (e.g., medicine, law, engineering). The historical evolution of management (See Appendix I) suggests that the field is fragmented and filled with formidable obstacles. There is a traditional division between theory, research and practice. There is also the prevalent debate between those who support professionalization and their opponents. Professionalization advocates emphasize the universality and transferability of managerial knowledge, skills, and competencies. Critics stress that the context-specific nature of management practice limits its transferability.

Whether management can or will ever become a profession doesn't answer a relevant question: Should managers behave professionally in managing assets? We believe that managers must behave more professionally. A starting point in managing more professionally is to apply the guidelines in this book.

Although the future of management is uncertain in terms of professionalization, stature, and respect, there is likely to be continuing debate about the value of professionalization. The guidelines in this book offer a starting point for testing different viewpoints. The prevailing public climate appears to be receptive to a more professional state of management. The social, moral, and economic dilemmas that managers face seem to require a break from doing the work of management as it has been done throughout history. The journey to increasing managerial professionalism requires that managers, educators, and researchers work more closely together to produce guidelines that can be applied, tested, modified, and unapologetically discarded if and when better evidence becomes available.

Afterword

APPENDIX A
TIMELINE OF
MANAGEMENT

The seeds of management were planted long ago, largely out of military necessity. Organizing and directing large groups of people to perform difficult and often distasteful tasks required the development of the most basic (though, by today's standards, not always ethical) management methods. As civilizations progressed, military methods of management were borrowed by burgeoning enterprises competing in increasingly mature and open markets.

Then came the industrial revolution. The industrial revolution launched the growth of management knowledge on an accelerating path that continues to this day. As knowledge of management grew and found application in industry, so too did the efficiency and productivity of organizations that adopted them. In the early part of the 20th century, the sheer volume of knowledge (as measured by the number of publications, institutions, theories and research) necessitated the creation of formal education and credentialing programs. By the middle part of the 20th century, the volume of knowledge was such as to justify MBA and doctoral programs. Today, many advocate that managers should pursue additional post-graduate certification or be required to participate in continuing education. One thing is certain; the acceleration in growth is not ebbing—as is evident in the timeline.

What are practicing managers to do? How can they discern legitimate theory and practice from fad and speculation? How can they ensure that their management practice is sound and keep up with new findings and developments in the field? We believe the development of guidelines like the ones in this book to be the only viable long-term solution.

Pre-Systematic Management
500 BC – 1830s

500 BC - Sun Tzu writes *The Art of War*, introducing strategies for organizing troops, maintaining morale, and achieving victory in battle.

390 AD - Vegetius writes *The Military Institutions of the Romans*, emphasizing discipline and setting the framework for the organization of the modern division.

1525 - Machiavelli writes *The Prince*, providing guidance on leadership and political strategy.

1776 - Adam Smith writes *The Wealth of Nations*, advancing concepts of the division of labor and job specialization.

500 BC - 1830s

A

Systematic Management
1830s – 1880

1760s to 1860s - Industrial revolution sweeps across Europe and the United States.

1832 - Charles Babbage writes *On the Economy of Machinery and Manufactures*, expanding Smith's work on the division of labor by proposing that specialization is as relevant to mental work as physical work.

Systematic Management

Emphasized economic controls, proper staffing, standardized techniques, and uninterrupted production.

Contributors include Babbage, Owen and Ure.

1830s – 1880

A

A

Scientific Management
1880s - 1900s

1880s - Taylor conducts seminal experiments at Midvale Steel Company on efficiency in the factory.

1911 - Taylor writes *The Principles of Scientific Management*, Consolidating the best ideas and practices into a single, overarching philosophy.

Scientific Management

Emphasized scientific analysis and research of work, its elements, standards and rates. Advocated use of scientific method for selection, training and development of employees. Presented the notion of shared responsibility between managers, and introduced time and motion studies.

Contributors include Barth, Emerson, Frank & Lillian Gilbreth, Gantt, Munsterberg, and Taylor.

Bureaucratic Management
1900s – 1915

1913 - Max Weber writes *The Theory of Social and Economic Organizations*, proposed principals and criteria for the ideal bureaucracy.

Bureaucratic Management

Emphasized bureaucratic structures to create stability, efficiency, and effectiveness. Key concepts of ideal bureaucracy included specialization of labor, formal rules and procedures, apply rules to everyone equally, well-defined hierarchy, career advancement based on merit.

Contributors include Michels and Weber.

1900s – 1915

A

Administrative Management
1915 – 1930s

1916 - Henri Fayol writes *General and Industrial Management*, proposing 5 functions and 14 principles of management.

Administrative Management

Emphasized management as a profession that can be learned. Examined management from the perspective of managers and executives responsible for coordinating the activities of diverse groups and units across organizations. Proposed that a request or directive should observe the chain of command.

Contributors include Barnard, Fyol, Gulick, Mooney, Reilly, Simon, and Urwick.

1915 – 1930s

A

Human Relations Management
1930s – 1950s

1927–1933 - Hawthorne studies find that human factors are often more important than environmental conditions in achieving increased productivity.

1940s - Tavistock coal mining studies that the introduction of new performance-improving technology disrupted social relationships among employees and actually reduced productivity.

1954 - Maslow publishes *Motivation and Personality*, proposing the "hierarchy of needs" theory.

Human Relations Management

Utilized the behavioral sciences to explain and illustrate how managers could motivate, lead, reward, and develop employees more effectively.

Contributors include Bamforth, Dickson, Follett, Maslow, Mayo, McGregor, Roethlsberger, and Trist.

1930s – 1950s

A

Quantitative and Systems Management
1950s – 1980s

1940s Mathematical and statistical modeling techniques developed during World War II are applied to industry after the war.

1950s - Deming promotes the use of statistical process control, laying the foundation for modern TQM.

1954 - Drucker writes *The Practice of Management*, proposing the 5 basic roles of managers.

1963 - J. Stacey Adams writes "Towards an Understanding of Inequity," contributing to the development of organizational justice models.

1967 - Fiedler writes *A Theory of Leadership Effectiveness*, laying the foundation for the situational leadership and contingency management movements.

1967 - Lawrence and Lorsch conduct the *Plastic Industry Study*, laying the foundation for contingency management.

1969–1973 - The Topeka Pet Food Plant experiments lays a foundation for the self-management movement.

Systems Management

Considered an organization to be an open or closed system. Introduced the view that an organization's environment must be taken into consideration in making decisions.

Contributors include Drucker, Emery, Kahn, Katz, Senge, von Bertalanffy.

Quantitative Management

Placed emphasis on using the scientific method and various analytical tools to make better financial, inventory, transportation, purchasing, selection, and forecasting decisions.

Contributors include Ackoff, Asby, Churchman, Forrester, Kuhn, McKinsey, Morganstern, and von Neumann.

Modern Management
1980s – Present

1982 - Peters and Waterman write *In Search of Excellence*, popularizing the use of management research to discover factors of excellence in successful organizations for a practitioner audience.

1988 - *Managing the Knowledge Assets Symposium* lays a foundation for the Knowledge Management movement.

1990 - Senge writes *The Fifth Discipline*, proposing the concept of "learning organization."

1991 - U.S. government institutes Federal Sentencing Guidelines, attempting to advance ethics, justice, and fair practice in business.

1993 - Hammer and Champy write *Re-Engineering the Corporation*, proposing radical versus incremental organizational change around customer needs.

1990s–2000s - Numerous corporate scandals reduce public confidence in management and governance.

Total Quality Management

Emphasized the concepts of quality, process control, quality assurance and quality improvement.

Contributors include Crosby, Deming, and Juran.

Knowledge Management

The value of knowledge as a vital organizational resource is recognized. Managers should cultivate a learning culture in which organizational members systematically gather, store, and share, knowledge with others.

Contributors include Amidon, Nonaka, Polanyi, Senge, Sveiby, Takeuchi, an Wiig.

Self Management

Employees are empowered to design, control, coordinate, and lead their workflow, interactions and performance systems. Intended to put dignity, sensitivity, and meaning into the job, the team, and the organizational system.

Contributors include Manz and Sims.

Re-Engineering

Focuses on organizing or radically, re-organizing around customer needs. The organization typically changes the structure, distribution system, human relations approach, and marketing employed to deliver products and services.

Seminal contributors include Champy and Hammer.

Situational Leadership

Proposes that effective leader behaviors vary from situation to situation. A leader analyzes the situation, selects the key factors, and then makes a decision on how to proceed.

Contributor include Fiedler, Grain, House, and Vroom.

Contingency Management

Emphasized in If-Then model. There is no perfect way to manage.

Contributors include Burns, Drucker, Lawrence, Lorsch, Stalker and Woodward.

Organizational Justice

Emphasizes fairness in the application of motivation, reward, performance review and feedback, and leadership interaction programs The fairness deals with perceptions, emotions, and the sense of value employees feel with regard to their contribution to their team and organization.

Contributors include Adams, Colquitt, Cropanzo, Greenberg, and Thibaut.

APPENDIX B
FREQUENTLY ASKED
QUESTIONS

If I disagree with a guideline, what should I do?

If you believe a guideline to be in error and have good evidence to support your belief, we recommend that you disregard the guideline and contact us by email at research@ams-institute.com with your reasoning. Submissions of this type will be considered for future editions of GFEM and full credit for the submission will be acknowledged in the book if the submission is used. If you believe a guideline is generally correct but not applicable to a particular situation, we would recommend discussing your reasoning with others in your organization. If there is consensus that a guideline does not apply, document your reasoning and disregard the guideline. Otherwise, we recommend following the guidelines as written.

My company does not follow a number of the guidelines in this book. How can I get them to follow more of them?

Organizational change takes time. We recommend introducing GFEM to the leadership in your area of the organization. If they are receptive, propose a pilot program to institute a select set of guidelines. Set clear goals and monitor the progress of implementation. Expand the effort as appropriate.

How do guidelines fit in with the "management is an art" school of thought?

By way of analogy, think of the guidelines in this book as rules of grammar. Knowing the rules of grammar will not, by itself, make you a great writer. Similarly, knowing the guidelines for management will not, by itself, make you a great manager. However, great writers know and follow the rules of grammar, and disregard them only when there is some compensating merit. Great managers should do likewise with the guidelines for management. The "art" of being a great writer is what occurs within and around the grammar. The "art" of being a great manager is what occurs within and around the guidelines for management.

What are the differences between "guidelines," "standards," and "best practices"?

"Standards" are practices that ought to be followed all of the time without exception. They are usually prescribed by industry associations, regulations, or internal policies. "Guidelines" are practices that ought to be followed most of the time. They are usually based on empirical research (or strong evidence) and are generalizable across most environments. "Best practices" are practices that have been observed to be effective in a particular environment. They may or may not be generalizable to other environments.

I noticed that the guidelines have index numbers. Why?

The guidelines have been indexed for convenient reference. The goal is to enable managers to support or contradict policies and practices through a simple and precise means of annotation.

Why is the book organized into just three categories (Direction, Execution, and People) and not into more categories as in other textbooks?

During the course of doing research for this book, we were surprised at the lack of consensus regarding a basic definition of management. When managers can't define what they are supposed to be doing, it should come as no surprise that they are not doing it. The organization of the book is designed to help managers focus on those areas that are critical to high-performance management: direction, execution, and people.

Why are guidelines for senior management (e.g., 1.3 Governance) put in the same book as guidelines for front-line personnel (e.g., 2.1 Process)?

It is to the benefit of everyone in the organization to know how his or her organization should be managed. Line-level managers may never be involved at the governance level of an organization, and many executives may never be involved at the execution level of an organization. In both cases, however, it is fruitful for these different levels of management to have a basic understanding of how these other areas of the organization should be managed. This helps all managers and employees to understand the organization as an integrated whole, which in turn helps to promote a culture of solidarity and healthy skepticism.

I do not agree that leadership is a subset of management. Why are leadership guidelines in a book on management?

It has been said that management is about doing things right, and leadership is about doing the right things. This is a good distinction. However, the practical reality in most organizations is that the management has the power. If managers do not have the capacity to lead they will not be able to foster leadership within the ranks. This is the fast track to a leaderless organization. So the short answer to the question is that for all practical purposes, leadership is *effectively* a subset of management in most organizations, and why we included it in this book.

Many of the guidelines are broad (e.g., 3.4.10). How can such broad guidelines be applied in a real-world work environment?

Guidelines such as 3.4.10 are primarily useful for raising awareness of behaviors and practices that are key to achieving high levels of performance. This awareness can help prevent or interrupt dysfunctional behaviors and practices before they become costly, and can play an important role in training, performance feedback, and project debriefs.

FAQ

B

There is a guideline that says to embrace management fads with caution (1.1.7). How do I know this book isn't just another management fad?

The foundation of GFEM is the scientific method. The guidelines in this book are the product of the best efforts of leading researchers, educators, and practitioners to convey what is presently known about good management practice. As the state of this knowledge becomes more complete and accurate over time, so too will the guidelines. It is our position that acting in accordance with the best available evidence is not—and never will be—a fad.

I think guidelines like these would be useful in other areas of my business—for example, sales. Are there any other guideline books in development for other subject areas?

A number of Guidelines for Excellence® books are under development in other business-related subject areas. For more information regarding books in this series, you can visit our Web site at www.ams-institute.com.

Is there any evidence that companies that follow these guidelines will do better than those that don't?

Each guideline makes this claim implicitly or explicitly, and cites some of the relevant evidence in the references section of this book. There also appears to be a clear positive correlation between the number of guidelines followed by an organization and their long-term financial performance. Additional research on the impact of guidelines adoption is ongoing, and will be made available on the AMSI Web site when complete.

My company wants to adopt GFEM, but we don't know where to begin. We can't possibly adopt them all at once. Any suggestions?

We would recommend assembling teams within the organization to review and select 7-10 high-impact guidelines for implementation per quarter. This is a visible and action-oriented process for educating the organization about management excellence while simultaneously improving the practice of the organization. The team should set specific implementation goals and review the progress of adoption on a regular basis.

Are you claiming that everything that is known about management is summarized in these guidelines?

Our claim is that a significant proportion of the actionable knowledge in management is represented by these guidelines.

In the Foreword, you state that a person who knowingly disregards a guideline is conducting "malpractice." Isn't this a bit strong?

It is strong, but we believe it is accurate. To knowingly disregard methods that are based on the best available evidence without good reason is, by definition, malpractice; it is a potentially injurious disservice to shareholders, employees, managers, and customers.

It seems like you think managers should just be automatons that follow these rules. Doesn't this approach dehumanize management?

If anything, following guidelines humanizes, not dehumanizes, management. Guidelines provide a necessary structure for improving individual, team, and organizational performance—i.e., to make people and organizations more successful in achieving their goals. This structure liberates managers from expending energy on the aspects of management that are relatively known and fixed, and enables them to focus more on the intangible aspects or "art" of good management. To dismiss such a structure for no good reason is at best poor management, and at worst malpractice.

Do guidelines apply to small companies as well as large? Start-ups?

The guidelines apply to most organizations. Smaller organizations—especially start-ups—will likely not have the many of the management structures in place to apply some of the guidelines (e.g., 1.3 Governance). In such cases, practitioners need to use their judgment in assessing the applicability of the guidelines and adopt accordingly.

Some of the guidelines are based more on common sense than on scientific research (e.g., 2.1.8). Why are they in the book?

The simple answer is people commonly don't follow them, and they are essential aspects of a high-performance management. The evidence supporting guidelines includes research, logic, common sense, best practices, and expert opinion, in varying combinations—it is not limited to scientific research.

I am planning on having my staff adopt GFEM. Is it okay for them to tailor some of the guidelines to better meet our specific needs, or should they be left "as is"?

This is an appropriate practice as long as the material aspects of the guidelines are not changed. For example, guideline "3.4.6 Share the rewards of success with all employees" could be changed to "3.4.6 Share the rewards of success with all team members" in order to reflect an organization's preference for the term "team member" over "employee." It would not be appropriate, however, to change the guideline to "3.4.6 Share the rewards of success with all team members" when referring to a local adoption of the guidelines within an organization, since this materially changes the scope of the guideline.

My company adopted Six Sigma and it created a bureaucratic nightmare. Won't adopting these guidelines create the same kinds of problems?

If the guidelines are implemented properly, the total amount of bureaucracy in the organization will be reduced. This is not to say that there will not be a local introduction of some bureaucracy to the organization as a result of some of the guidelines. For example, "2.1.10 Create and follow an explicit agenda at every meeting" creates additional bureaucracy for organizations currently not engaged in such practice. But, much like the necessary healthy fats and carbohydrates in diets, this is "good" bureaucracy—the resulting gains in productivity outweigh the costs.

FAQ

B

REFERENCES

Know what business you are in.
1.1.1

Drucker, P. (1954). The practice of management. New York: HarperCollins.

Levitt, T. (1960, July/August). Marketing myopia. *Harvard Business Review*, 38(4), 45–56.

Nohria, N., Joyce, W., & Roberson, B. (2003, July). What really works. *Harvard Business Review*, 1–12.

Do not manage organizations like investment portfolios.
1.1.2

Lubatkin, M., & Chatterjee, S. (1994, August). Extending modern portfolio theory into the domain of corporate diversification: Does it apply? *The Academy of Management Journal*, 37(1), 109–136.

Manage for the long term—even when it hurts in the short term.
1.1.3

Appelbaum, E., & Batt, R. (1994). The new American workplace. Ithaca, NY: ILR.

Cascio, W. F. (2002). Strategies for responsible restructuring. *The Academy of Management Executive*, 16(3), 80–91.

Collins, J. C., & Porras, J. I. (1994). Built to last: Successful habits of visionary companies. New York: HarperBusiness.

Khurana, R. (2002). Searching for a corporate savior: The irrational quest for charismatic CEOs, Princeton: Princeton University Press.

Rumelt, R., Schendel, D., & Tece, D. (1991). Strategic management and economics. *Strategic Management Journal*, 12, 5–29.

Seglin, J. L. (2003, Spring). The myopia of bad behavior. *MIT Sloan Management Review*, 96.

Favor offense over defense.
1.1.4

Chen, M., Smith, K. G., & Grimm, C. M. (1992). Action characteristics as predictors of competitive responses. *Management Science*, 38(3), 439–455.

Ferrier, W. J. (2001, August). Navigating the competitive landscape: the drivers and consequences of competitive aggressiveness. *The Academy of Management Journal*, 44(4), 858–877.

Makadok, R. (1998, July). Can first-mover and early-mover advantages be sustained in an industry with low barriers to entry/initiation? *Strategic Management Journal*, 19(7), 683–696.

Smith, K. G., Ferrier, W. J., & Grimm, C. M. (2001). King of the hill: Dethroning the industry leader. *The Academy of Management Executive*, 15(2), 59–70.

1.1.5   Respond faster than competitors.

Ali, A., Krapfel, R., & LaBahn, D. (1995). Product innovativeness and entry strategy: Impact on cycle time and break-even time. *Journal of Product Innovation Management*, 12(1), 54–69.

Leonard-Barton, D. (1992, Summer). Core capabilities and core rigidities: A paradox in managing new product development. *Strategic Management Journal*, 13(5), 111–126.

Smith, K. G., Ferrier, W. J., & Grimm, C. M. (2001). King of the hill: Dethroning the industry leader. *The Academy of Management Executive*, 15(2), 59–70.

1.1.6   Use the competition as a source of free research and development.

Briody, D., & Moskowitz, E. (2001, October 1). Dell: The antitechnology company. *Red Herring*.

Christensen, C., Craig, T., & Hart, S. (2001, March/April). The great disruption. *Foreign Affairs*, 80(2), 80–95.

Porter, M. (1998). Competitive strategy: Technique for analyzing industries and competitors. New York: The Free Press.

1.1.7   Embrace management fads with caution.

Abrahamson, E. (1991, July). Management fads and fashions: The diffusion and rejection of innovations. *Academy of Management Review*, 16(3), 586–612.

Boyett, J. H., & Boyett, J. T. (2000). The guru guide: The best ideas of the top management thinkers. New York: John Wiley & Sons.

Clark, T., & Salaman, G. (1988, March). Telling tales: Management gurus' narratives and the construction of organizational identity. *Journal of Management Studies*, 25(2), 137–161.

Cole, R. E. (1999). Managing quality fads: How American business learned to play the quality game. New York: American Society for Quality.

1.1.8   Act differently than the competition.

Collins, J. (2001). Good to great: Why some companies make the leap . . . and others don't. New York: HarperCollins.

Hambrick, D. C., & Fredrickson, J. W. (2001, November). Are you sure you have a strategy? *The Academy of Management Executive*, 15(4), 48–59.

Porter, M. E. (1996, November/December). What is strategy? *Harvard Business Review*, 74(6), 61–78.

Rijamampianina, R., Abratt, R., & February, Y. (2003, April). A framework for concentric diversification through sustainable competitive advantage. *Management Decision*, 41(4), 362–371.

Grow the core business. Phase out noncore business. 1.1.9

Collins, J. (2001). Good to great: Why some companies make the leap . . . and others don't. New York: HarperCollins.

Sonnenfeld, J. (2002, June 12). Expanding without managing. *The New York Times*.

Outsource noncore business functions only. 1.1.10

Bardhan, A. D., & Kroll, C. A. (2003, Fall). The new wave of outsourcing. Research Report: Fisher Center for Real Estate and Urban Economics, University of California, Berkeley.

Barthélemy, J. (2003, May). The seven deadly sins of outsourcing. *The Academy of Management Executive*, 17(2), 87–100.

Bettis, R. A., Bradley, S. P., & Hamel, G. (1992, February). Outsourcing and industrial decline. *The Academy of Management Executive*, 6(1), 7–22.

Gilley, K. M., & Rasheed, A. (2000). Making more by doing less: An analysis of outsourcing and its effects on firm performance. *Journal of Management*, 26(4), 736–790.

Consult with key people in the organization when creating strategic plans. 1.1.11

Kaplan, S., & Beinhocker, E. D. (2003, Winter). The real value of strategic planning. *MIT Sloan Management Review*, 44(2), 71–76.

Kim, S. (2002, March/April). Participative management and job satisfaction: Lessons for management leadership. *Public Administration Review*, 62(2), 231–241.

Larsen, P., Tonge, R., & Ito, M. (2000, December). Managing the strategic planning process: A comparative analysis between high-growth medium-sized enterprises and the general business population. *Journal of Applied Management Studies*, 9(2), 275–282.

O'Regan, N., & Ghobadian, A. (2002). Effective strategic planning in small and medium sized firms. *Management Decision*, 40(3), 663–671.

Regularly revisit, review, and revise strategic plans. 1.1.12

Beinhocker, E. D., & Kaplan, S. (2002) Tired of strategic planning? The *McKinsey Quarterly*, 2, 48–57.

Liedtka, J. (2000, April). Strategic planning as a contributor to strategic change: A generative model. *European Management Journal*, 18(2), 195–206.

Oliver, R. W. (2000, March/April). The real-time toolbox. *Journal of Business Strategy*, 21(2), 7–10.

1.1.13   **Incorporate multiple scenarios and contingencies in strategic plans.**

Andersen, E. (2003, September). Be prepared for the unforeseen. *Journal of Contingencies and Crisis Management*, 11(3), 129–131.

Miller, C. C., & Cardinal, L. B. (1994). Strategic planning and firm performance: A synthesis of more than two decades of research. *The Academy of Management Journal*, 37(6), 1649–1665.

Mintzberg, H. (1993, Fall). The pitfalls of strategic planning. *California Management Review*, 36(1), 32–47.

Roney, C. W. (2003). Planning for strategic contingencies. *Business Horizons*, 46(2), 35–42.

Schwartz, P. (1996). The art of the long view: Planning for the future in an uncertain world. New York: Doubleday.

van der Heijden, K. (1996). Scenarios: The art of strategic conversation. New York: John Wiley & Sons.

1.1.14   **Apply the 4+2 formula.**

Joyce, W., Nohria, N., and Roberson, B. (2003). What (really) works: The 4+2 formula for sustained business success. HarperBusiness.

1.1.15   **Do not hesitate to cannibalize existing products.**

Hill, C.W.L. and Rothaermel, F.T. (2003, April). "The performance of incumbent firms in the face of radical technological innovation." *Academy of Management Review*, 28(2), 257–274.

Joyce, W., Nohria, N., and Roberson, B. (2003). *What (really) works: The 4+2 formula for sustained business success.* HarperBusiness.

Kaplan, S. and Foster, S. (2001). *Creative destruction: Why companies that are built to last underperform the market—and how to successfully transform them.* Currency-Doubleday.

Kirkpatrick, D. (1994, May 16). "Intel Goes for Broke." *Fortune*, 62–68.

Neff, M.C. and Shanklin, W.L. (1997, May/June) "Creative destruction as a market strategy." *Research Technology Management*, 40(3), 33–40.

1.2.1   **Cultivate a quiet and focused leadership culture.**

Badaracco, Jr., J. L. (2002). Leading quietly: An unorthodox guide to doing the right thing. Boston: Harvard Business School Press.

Collins, J. (2001). Good to great: Why some companies make the leap . . . and others don't. New York: HarperCollins.

Sample, S. (2001). The contrarian's guide to leadership. San Francisco: Jossey-Bass.

1.2.2   **Focus on the critical 20 percent when making decisions.**

Gersick, C. J. G. (1989, June). Marking time: Predictable transitions in task groups. *The Academy of Management Journal*, 32(2), 274–309.

Katz, N., & Koenig, G. (2001, August). Sports teams as a model for workplace teams: Lessons and liabilities. *The Academy of Management Executive*, 15(3), 56–69.

Koch, R. (1999). The 80/20 individual. New York: Currency.

Communicate long-term goals in person.   **1.2.3**

Frost, C. (1986). Participative ownership: A competitive necessity. *New Management*, 3(4), 44–49.

Guffey, W. R., & Nienhaus, B. J. (2002, Spring). Determinants of employee support for the strategic plan of a business unit. *SAM Advanced Management Journal*, 67(2), 23–30.

Lengel, R. H., & Daft, R. L. (1988). The selection of communication media as an executive skill. *The Academy of Management Executive*, 2(3), 225–232.

Miniace, J. N., & Falter, E. (1996). Communication: A key factor in strategy implementation. *Planning Review*, 24(1), 26–29.

Schweiger, D. M., & Denisi, A. S. (1991). Communication with employees following a merger: A longitudinal field experiment. *The Academy of Management Journal*, 34(1), 110–135.

Wander around.   **1.2.4**

Ackerman, L. S. (1982, Summer). Transition management: An in-depth look at managing complex change. *Organizational Dynamics*, 11(1), 46–66.

Amsbary, J. H. (1991, Spring). Improving administrator/nurse communication: A case study of "management by wandering around." *Journal of Business Communication*, 28(2), 101–112.

Peters, T .J., & Waterman, R. H. (1982). In search of excellence: Lessons from America's best run companies. New York: Harper and Row.

Trueman, W. (1991). CEO isolation and how to fight it. *Canadian Business*, 64(7), 28–33.

Create a personal "anticipation registry."   **1.2.5**

Finkelstein, S. (2003). Why smart executives fail: And what you can learn from their mistakes. New York: Portfolio.

Krass, P. (1998). The book of leadership wisdom: Classic writings by legendary business leaders. New York: John Wiley & Sons.

Create a sense of healthy urgency.   **1.2.6**

Burke, W. W. (2002). Organization change: Theory and practice. Thousand Oaks, CA: Sage Publications.

Kotter, J. P. (1996). Leading change. Boston: Harvard Business School Press.

Rogers, E. M. (1995). Diffusion of innovation. New York: The Free Press.

Sims, R. R. (2002). Changing the way we manage change. Westport, CT: Quorum.

1.2.7   **Apply policies consistently to all levels of management.**

Bennis, W. (1993). Learning some basic truisms about leadership: Emerging strategies for leadership and organizational change. In Ray, M., & Rinzler, A. (Eds.). *New paradigm in business*. New York: Jeremy P. Tarcher/Perigree Books.

Hegarty, W. H., & Sims, H. P. (1979, June). Organizational philosophy, policies, and objectives related to unethical decision behavior: A laboratory experiment. *Journal of Applied Psychology*, 64(3), 331–338.

1.2.8   **Set challenging but attainable goals.**

Locke, E. A., & Latham, G. P. (1984). Goal setting: A motivational technique that works. Englewood Cliffs, NJ: Prentice Hall.

Shalley, C. E., Oldham, G. R., & Porac, J. F. (1987, September). Effects of goal difficulty, goal-setting method, and expected external evaluation on intrinsic motivation. *The Academy of Management Journal*, 30(3), 553–563.

1.2.9   **Favor reducing barriers over increasing pressure.**

Lewin, K. (1936). Principles of topological psychology. New York: McGraw-Hill.

Lewin, K. (1948). Resolving social conflicts, selected papers on group dynamics. Edited by Dorwin Cartwright. New York: Harper.

Lewin, K. (1951). Field theory in social science. New York: Harper.

Lewin, K. (1958). Group decision and social change. In Maccoby, E. E., Newcomb, T. M., & Hartley, E. L. (Eds.). *Readings in social psychology* (pp. 197–211). New York: Holt, Rinehart and Winston.

Welch, J., & Byrne, J. A. (2001). Jack: Straight from the gut. New York: Warner Books.

1.2.10   **Actively support training and development.**

Dutton, J. E., & Ashford, S. J. (1993). Selling issues to top management. *Academy of Management Review*, 18, 397–428.

Noe R. A., & Ford, J. K. (1992). Emerging issues and new directions for training research. In Ferris, G., & Rowland, K. (Eds.). *Research in personnel and human resources management*, 10 (pp. 345–384). Greenwich, CT: JAI Press.

Phillips, J. J. (1978, August). How to improve management support for supervisory training programs. *Training & Development Journal*, 32(8), 23–28.

Scott, W. R., & Meyer J. W. (1991). The rise of training programs in firms and agencies: An institutional perspective. In Staw, B., & Cummings, L. L. (Eds.). *Research in organizational behavior*, 13 (pp. 297–326). Greenwich, CT: JAI Press.

Yarnall, J. (1998). Line managers as career developers: rhetoric or reality? *Personnel Review*, 27(5), 378–395.

1.2.11   **Declare a "revolution" when radical change is required.**

Beer, M., & Nohria, N. (2000, May/June). Cracking the code of change. *Harvard Business Review*, 78(3), 133–141.

Huy, Q. N. (2001, September). In praise of middle managers. *Harvard Business Review*, 79(8), 73–39.

Khurana, R., & Nohria, N. (2000, March 15). The performance consequences of CEO turnover. Working Papers Series—Harvard Business School Division of Research. Retrieved January 25, 2004, from http://ssrn.com/abstract=219129

Miller, D., & Friesen, P. H. (1980). Momentum and revolution in organization adaptation. *The Academy of Management Journal*, 23(4), 591–614.

Wilkins, A. L., & Bristow, N. J. (1987, August). For successful organization culture: Honor your past. *The Academy of Management Executive*, 1(3), 221–229.

Avoid the "principal-principal" problem. **1.2.12**

Finkelstein, S. (2003). Why smart executives fail: And what you can learn from their mistakes. New York: Portfolio.

Create synergies in mergers and acquisitions. **1.2.13**

Finkelstein, S. (2003). Why smart executives fail: And what you can learn from their mistakes. New York: Portfolio.

Downsize in one dramatic event—not gradually. **1.2.14**

American Management Association. (1997). Corporate job creation, job elimination, and downsizing: Summary of key findings. New York: American Management Association.

Cascio, W. F. (1993, February). Downsizing: What do we know? What have we learned? *The Academy of Management Executive*, 7(1), 94–104.

Feldman, D. C., & Leana, C. R. (1994, Summer). Better practices in managing layoffs. *Human Resource Management*, 33(2), 239–260.

Use moral management as the primary leadership approach. **1.2.15**

Business Ethics Magazine. (1997). Business ethics award criteria. *Business Ethics*, 11(6), 8.

Carroll, A. B. (1987, March/April). In search of the moral manager. *Business Horizons*, 30(2), 7–15.

Carroll, A. B. (2001). Models of management morality for the new millennium. *Business Ethics Quarterly*, 11(2), 365–371.

Carroll, A. B. (2001). The moral leader: Essential for successful corporate citizenship. In Andriof, J., & McIntosh, M. (Eds.). *Perspectives on corporate citizenship* (pp 139–151). Sheffield, UK: Greenleaf Publishing Company.

Heenan, D. A. (1989, November/December). The downside of downsizing. *Journal of Business Strategy*, 10(6), 18–23.

Sikula, Sr., A. (1996). Concepts of moral management and moral maximization. *Ethics & Behavior*, 6(3), 181–188.

1.2.16 **Use coaching to enhance executive performance.**

Greco, J. (2001, March/April). Hey, coach! *Journal of Business Strategy*, 22(2), 28–31.

Kampa-Kokesch, S., & Anderson, M. Executive coaching: A comprehensive review of the literature. *Consulting Psychology Journal: Practice and Research*, 53, 205–228.

Kluger, A., & DeNisi, A. (1996). The effects of feedback interventions on performance: A historical review, meta-analysis and preliminary feedback theory. *Psychological Bulletin*, 119, 254–285.

McGovern, J., Lindermann, M., Vergara, M., Murphy, S., Baker, L., & Warrenfeltz, R. (2001). Maximizing the impact of executive coaching: Behavioral change, organizational outcomes, and return on investment. *The Manchester Review*, 6(1), 1–9.

Orenstein, R. L. (2002, September). Executive coaching. *Journal of Applied Behavioral Science*, 38(3), 355–374.

1.2.17 **Be empathetic.**

Cherniss, C., & Goleman, D. (2001). The emotionally intelligent workplace: How to select for, measure, and improve emotional intelligence in individuals, groups, and organizations. San Francisco: Jossey-Bass.

Feldman, D. A. (1999). The handbook of emotionally intelligent leadership: Inspiring others to achieve results. Leadership Performance Solutions.

Goleman, D. (1995). Emotional intelligence. New York: Bantam Books.

Massarik, F., & Weschler, I. R. (1959, Winter). Empathy revisited. *California Management Review*, 1(2), 36–46.

Settoon, R. P., & Mossholder, K. W. (2002, April). Relationship quality and relationship context as antecedents of person- and task-focused interpersonal citizenship behavior. *Journal of Applied Psychology*, 87(2), 255–267.

1.2.18 **Explain the reasons behind decisions honestly.**

Folger, R., & Skarlicki, D. P. (2001). Fairness as a dependent variable: Why tough times can lead to bad management. In Cropanzano, R. (Ed.). *Justice in the workplace: From theory to practice* (pp. 97–118). Mahwah, NJ: Erlbaum.

Kim, W. C., & Mauborgne, R. (2003, January). Fair process: Managing in the knowledge economy. *Harvard Business Review*, 81(1), 127–136.

Shaw, J. C., Wild, E., & Colquitt, J. A. (2003). To justify or excuse?: A meta-analytic review of the effects of explanations. *Journal of Applied Psychology*, 88(3), 444–458.

1.2.19 **Focus on meeting (not exceeding) customer expectations.**

Joyce, W., Nohria, N., and Roberson, B. (2003). *What (really) works: The 4+2 formula for sustained business success*. HarperBusiness.

Ensure that a majority of directors come from outside the organization.   **1.3.1**

Bainbridge, S. M. (1993, April). Independent directors and the ALI corporate governance project. *The George Washington Law Review*, 61(4), 1034–1083.

Monks, R. A. G., & Minow, N. (2001). Corporate governance (2nd ed.). Oxford: Blackwell Publishing.

Salmon, W. J., Lorsch, J. W., Donaldson, G., Pound, J., Conger, J., Finegold, D., Lawler III, E. E., Khurana, R., & Harvard Business School (2000). Harvard business review on corporate governance. Boston: Harvard Business School Press.

Westphal, J. D. (1999, February). Collaboration in the boardroom: Behavior and performance consequences of CEO-board social ties. *The Academy of Management Journal*, 42(1), 7–24.

Focus on oversight and not micromanagement.   **1.3.2**

Ashkenas, R. N., Ulrich, D., Jick, T., & Kerr, S. (2002). The boundaryless organization: Breaking the chains of organization structure. New York: John Wiley & Sons.

Strikwerda, J. (2003). An entrepreneurial model of corporate governance: Devolving powers to subsidiary boards. *Corporate Governance: International Journal of Business in Society*, 3(2), 38–57.

Develop formal codes of conduct that affirm ethical values and behavior.   **1.3.3**

Moorthy, R. S., De George, R. T., Donaldson T., Ellos, W. J., Solomon, R. C., & Textor, R. B. (1998). Uncompromising integrity: Motorola's global challenge. Schaumburg, IL: Motorola University Press.

Post, J. E., Preston, L. E., & Sachs, S. (2002). Redefining the corporation: Stakeholder management and organizational wealth. Stanford, CA: Stanford University Press.

Williams, O. F., (Ed.) (2000). Global codes of conduct: An idea whose time has come. Notre Dame, IN: University of Notre Dame Press.

Observe a zero tolerance policy regarding discrimination.   **1.3.4**

Greengard, S. (1999, May). Zero tolerance: Making it work. *Workforce*, 28–33

Hemphill, H. (1998, April 13). Combat harassment by starting with mind. *Business Insurance*, 16.

Katzenstein, M. F., & Reppy, J. (1999). Beyond zero tolerance. Lanham, MD: Rowman & Littlefield Publishing.

Milite, G. A., (1999, December). What you know about harassment can hurt you, too. *HR Focus*, 9–10.

Institute a formal process of evaluating board performance.   **1.3.5**

Conger, J. A., Lawler III, E. E., & Finegold, D. L. (2001). Corporate boards: New strategies for adding value at the top. San Francisco: Jossey-Bass.

Kaplan, R. S., & Norton, D. P. (1996). The balanced scorecard: Translating strategy into action. Boston: Harvard Business School Press.

Korn/Ferry International. (2002). U.S. 29th Annual board of directors study—Emerging Companies.

1.3.6   **Institute a formal process of evaluating organizational performance.**

Hillman, A. J., & Dalziel, T. Boards of directors and firms performance: Integrating agency and resource dependence perspectives. *Academy of Management Review*, 28(3), 383–396.

Olve, N. G., Wetter, M., & Roy, J. (2001). Performance drivers: A practical guide to using the balanced scorecard. New York: John Wiley & Sons.

1.3.7   **Appoint an audit committee comprised of independent directors.**

Alam, P., Meonske N., & Pearson, M. A. (2003, May). Financial reporting integrity: IMA members speak out. *Strategic Finance*, 84(11), 41–45.

Light, M. (2001). The Strategic Board: The step-by-step guide to high-impact governance. New York: John Wiley & Sons.

Rezaee, Z., Olibe, K. O., & Minmier, G. (2003). Improving corporate governance: The role of audit committee disclosures. *Managerial Auditing Journal*, 18(6/7), 530–537.

1.3.8   **Enable directors to have access to managers below CEO level.**

Colley, J. L., Logan, G., Stettinius, W., Snyder, R., & Doyle, J. L. (2003). Corporate governance: The McGraw-Hill executive MBA series. New York: McGraw-Hill.

Lechem, B. (2002). Chairman of the board: A practical guide. New York: John Wiley & Sons.

1.3.9   **Institute a formal compliance program.**

Cavanagh, T. E. (2003). Corporate security management: Organization and spending since 9/11. New York: The Conference Board.

Joseph, J. (2002, Fall). Integrating business ethics and compliance programs: A study of ethics officers in leading organizations. *Business and Society Review*, 107(3), 309–347.

Propper, E. M., (2000). Corporate fraud investigations and compliance programs. Dobbs Ferry, New York: Oceana Publications.

1.3.10   **Establish a red-flag monitoring program.**

Collins, P. J., & Lawson, K. (1997, April). Implementing a portfolio sufficiency monitoring program. *Journal of Financial Planning*, 10(2), 86–90.

Dimma, W. A. (2002). Excellence in the boardroom: Best practices in corporate directorship. New York: John Wiley & Sons.

Garratt, B., & Monks, R. A. G. (2003). Thin on top: Why corporate governance matters and how to measure, manage, and improve board performance. Yarmouth, ME: Nicholas Brealey Publishing.

Distribute background information for upcoming board meetings in advance.   **1.3.11**

Dimma, W. A. (2002). Excellence in the boardroom: Best practices in corporate directorship. New York: John Wiley & Sons.

Lechem, B. (2002). Chairman of the board: A practical guide. New York: John Wiley & Sons.

Link director compensation to board performance.   **1.3.12**

Conger, J. A., Finegold, D. L., & Lawler III, E. E. (1998). Appraising boardroom performance. *Harvard Business Review*, 76(1), 136–148.

Dalton, D. R., & Dailey, C. (2001, January). Director stock compensation: An invitation to a conspicuous conflict of interests? *Business Ethics Quarterly*, 11(1), 81–108.

Powell, B. A. (2003, September/October). Which directors will get a raise in 2004. *Corporate Board Member*, 10–15.

Russell Reynolds Associates. (2001). 2000–2001 Board practices survey: The structure and compensation of boards of directors of U.S. public companies. New York: Russell Reynolds.

Provide strategic direction while also overseeing strategy implementation.   **1.3.13**

Hillman, A., & Dalziel, T. (2003, July). Boards of directors and firm performance: Integrating agency and resource dependence perspectives. *Academy of Management Review*, 28(3), 383–396.

Moreau, G. (2003, May/June). Fixing corporate boards. *Across the Board*, 40(3), 45–48.

Establish a policy addressing whistle-blower protection.   **1.3.14**

Brodsky, D. M., & Connelly, B. E. (2003, January/February). New whistle-blower protection liability under the Sarbanes-Oxley Act. *Corporate Governance Advisor*, 11(1), 26–29.

Joel III, L. G. (1996). Every employee's guide to the Law. New York: Pantheon Books.

Stout, L. A., & Blair M. M. (2001, Summer). Director accountability and the mediating role of the corporate board. *Washington University Law Quarterly*, 79(2), 403–447.

Appoint a nominating committee to screen and select director candidates.   **1.3.15**

Johnson, J. L., Daily, C. M., & Ellstrand, A. E. (1996). Boards of directors: A review and research agenda. *Journal of Management*, 22(3), 409–438.

Seymann, M., & Rosenbaum, M. (2003). The governance game: Restoring boardroom excellence and credibility in corporate America. Boston: Aspatore Books.

Limit the number of boards on which directors can serve.   **1.3.16**

Carver, J., & Carver, M. M. (1996). CarverGuide 1, Basic principles of policy governance. San Francisco: Jossey-Bass.

Ward, R. D. (2000). Improving corporate boards: The boardroom insider guidebook. New York: John Wiley & Sons.

Zajac, E. J., & Westphal, J. D. (1996). Director reputation, CEO-board power, and board interlocks. *Administrative Science Quarterly*, 41(3). 507–529.

1.3.17   Establish and enforce a minimum level of board meeting attendance.

Blair, M. M., & MacLaury, B. K. (1995). Ownership and control: Rethinking corporate governance for the twenty-first century. Washington, DC: The Brookings Institute.

Forbes, D. P., & Milliken, F. J. (1999). Cognition and corporate governance: Understanding board of directors as strategic decision-making groups. *Academy of Management Review*, 24(3), 489–505.

Morck, R. W., Schleifer, A., & Vishny, R. W. (1989). Alternative mechanisms for corporate control. *The American Economic Review*, 79, 842–852.

Root, S. J. (2000). Beyond Coso: Internal control to enhance corporate governance. New York: John Wiley & Sons.

1.3.18   Establish and maintain a CEO succession plan.

Cohn, J., & Khurana, R. (2003, May). How to succeed at CEO succession planning. *Directorship*, 29(5), 10–15.

Fredrickson, J. W., Hambrick, D. C., & Baumrin, S. (1988). A model of CEO dismissal. *Academy of Management Review*, 13, 255–270.

Shen, W., & Cannella, Jr., A. A. (2002). Power dynamics within top management and their impacts on CEO dismissal followed by inside succession. *The Academy of Management Journal*, 45(6), 1195–1206.

1.3.19   Provide corporate governance policies to shareholders.

Clampitt, P. G. (2001). Communicating for managerial effectiveness. Thousand Oaks, CA: Sage Publications.

Jensen, M. C., & Warner, J. B. (1988, January/March). The distribution of power among corporate managers, shareholders, and directors. *Journal of Finance & Economics*, 20, 3–24.

1.3.20   Provide training for directors.

Elliott, A. L., & Schroth, R. J. (2002). How companies lie. New York: Crown Business Publications.

Shaw, J. (2003). Corporate governance and risk: A systems approach. New York: John Wiley & Sons.

1.3.21   Ensure that directors have input regarding board and committee meeting agendas.

Baysinger, B. D., & Hoskisson, R. E. (1990). The composition of boards of directors and strategic control: Effects on corporate strategy. *Academy of Management Review*, 15(1), 72–87.

Dailey, C. M. (1995). An empirical examination of the relationship between CEOs and directors. *Journal of Business Strategies*, 12, 50–68.

Limit the number of directors to between 8 and 14.   **1.3.22**

Dalton, D., Daily, C., Johnson, J., & Ellstrand, A. (1999). Number of directors and financial performance: A meta-analysis. *The Academy of Management Journal*, 42(6), 674–686.

National Association of Corporate Directors & the Center for Board Leadership. (1999, October). 1999–2000 public company governance survey. Washington, DC: National Association of Corporate Directors.

Sherman, H., & Chaganti, R. (1998). Corporate governance and the timeliness of change: Reorientation in 100 American firms. Westport, CT: Quorum.

Appoint different people as chairperson and CEO.   **1.3.23**

Daily, C. M., & Schwenk, C. (1996). Chief executive officers, top management teams, and board of directors: Congruent or countervailing forces? *Journal of Management*, 22(2), 185–208.

Patricof, A. J., Henderson, D., Marcus, B., Smale, J. G., & Johnson, D. W. (1995, March/April). Redraw the line between the board and the CEO. *Harvard Business Review*, 73(2), 153–155, 158–164.

Rechner, P. L., & Dalton, D. R. (1991, February). CEO duality and organizational performance: A longitudinal analysis. *Strategic Management Journal*, 12(2), 155–160.

Salmon, W. J., Lorsch, J. W., Donaldson, G., Pound, J., Conger, J., Finegold, D., Lawler III, E. E., Khurana, R., & Harvard Business School. (2000). Harvard business review on corporate governance. Boston: Harvard Business School Press.

Adjust board meeting frequency to meet the needs of the organization.   **1.3.24**

Denis, D. J., & Sarin, A. (1999). Ownership and board structures in publicly traded corporations. *Journal of Financial Economics*, 52(2), 187–223.

Knox, S. (2002). The boardroom agenda: Developing the innovative organization. *Corporate Governance*, 2, 27–37.

Lorsch, J. W., & MacIver, E. A. (1989). Pawns or potentates: The reality of America's corporate boards. Boston: Harvard Business School Press.

Vafeas, N. (1999). Board meeting frequency and firm performance. *Journal of Financial Economics*, 53, 113–142.

Integrate stakeholder concerns into the mission and practice of the organization.   **1.3.25**

Accorsi, R., Apostolakis, G., & Zio, E. (1999, January). Prioritizing stakeholder concerns in environmental risk management. *Journal of Risk Research*, 2(1), 11–29.

Carroll, A. B., & Buchholtz, A. K. (2003). Business & society with Infotrac: Ethics and stakeholder management (5th ed.). Cincinnati: South-Western College Publishing Company.

The Clarkson Centre for Business Ethics. (1999). Principles of stakeholder management. Toronto, Canada: School of Management, University of Toronto.

Walker, S. F., & Marr, J. W. (2001). Stakeholder power: A winning plan for building stakeholder commitment and driving corporate growth. Cambridge, MA: Perseus Publishing.

1.3.26   Consider the interests of all stakeholders—not just managers and shareholders.

Blair, M. (2001). Corporate governance. In Smelser, N. J., & Baltes, P. B. (Eds.). *International encyclopedia of the social and behavioral sciences*, 4 (pp. 2797–2803). Amsterdam, NY: Elsevier.

Gregory, R., & Keeney, R. L. (1994, August). Creating policy alternatives using stakeholder values. *Management Science*, 40(8), 1035–1048.

Monks, R. A. G., & Minow, N. (2001). Corporate governance (2nd ed.). Oxford: Blackwell Publishing.

2.1.1   Measure performance in simple, nonintrusive ways.

Ashton, C. (1997). Strategic performance measurement. London, UK: Business Intelligence.

Kanji, G. K. (2002, August). Performance measurement system. *Total Quality Management*, 13(5), 715–728.

Kaplan, R. S., & Norton, D. P. (1992, January/February). The balanced scorecard—Measures that drive performance. *Harvard Business Review*, 70(1), 71–79.

Laufer, A. (1997). Simultaneous management: Managing projects in a dynamic environment. New York: AMACOM.

2.1.2   Build in evaluative guideposts for new ventures with long time horizons.

Buck, P. S. (1944). What America means to me. London: Meuthuen.

Finkelstein, S. (2003). Why smart executives fail: And what you can learn from their mistakes. New York: Portfolio.

2.1.3   Assign a representative group to make decisions when "buy-in" is key.

Janis, I. L. (1989). Crucial decisions: Leadership in policymaking and crisis management. New York: The Free Press.

Murnighan, J. K. (1981, February). Group decision making: What strategies should you use? *Management Review*, 70(2), 55–62.

Orlitzky, M., & Hirokawa, R. Y. (2001, June). To err is human, to correct for it divine: A meta-analysis of research testing the functional theory of group decision-making effectiveness. *Small Group Research*, 32(3), 313–341.

2.1.4   Assign an individual expert to make decisions when efficiency is key.

Brown, R. (1988). Group processes: Dynamics within and between groups. Oxford: Blackwell Publishers.

Diehl, M., & Stroebe, W. (1991, September). Productivity loss in idea generating groups: Tracking down the blocking effect. *Journal of Personality and Social Psychology*, 61(3), 392–403.

Determine the partitionability of tasks before adding resources.   **2.1.5**

Brooks, Jr., F. P. (1995). The mythical man-month: Essays on software engineering, anniversary edition. Boston: Addison-Wesley.

Ritualize the practice of project debriefings and self-evaluation.   **2.1.6**

Beck, K. (1999). Extreme programming. New York: Pearson Education.

Meredith, J. R., Mantel, S. J., & Mantel, Jr., S. J. (2002). Project management: A managerial approach. New York: John Wiley & Sons.

Schedule a "halftime" at the midpoint of projects.   **2.1.7**

Gersick, C. J. G. (1989, June). Marking time: Predictable transitions in task groups. *The Academy of Management Journal*, 32(2), 274–309.

Katz, N., & Koenig, G. (2001, August). Sports teams as a model of workplace teams: Lessons and liabilities. *The Academy of Management Executive*, 15(3), 56–69.

Keep written communications short and simple.   **2.1.8**

Churchill, W. (1940, August 9). Brevity: Memorandum by the prime minister. W.P.(G)(40) 211, 20.

Communicate important messages in multiple ways.   **2.1.9**

Fulk, J., & Boyd, B. (1991). Emerging theories of communication in organizations. *Journal of Management*, 17, 407–446.

Hartley, P., & Bruckmann, C. G. (2002). Business communication. London: Routledge.

Rice, R. E. (1993). Media appropriateness: Using social presence theory to compare traditional and new organizational media. *Human Communication Research*, 19(4), 451–484.

Create and follow an explicit agenda at every meeting.   **2.1.10**

Cohen, S. G., & Bailey, D. E. (1997). What makes teams work: Group effectiveness research from the shop floor to the executive suite. *Journal of Management*, 23(3), 239–290.

Katzenbach, J. R., & Smith D. K. (1993). The wisdom of teams: Creating the high-performance organization. Boston: Harvard University Press.

Document meeting events and action items.   **2.1.11**

Risser, R. (1993). Stay out of court. Englewood Cliffs, NJ: Prentice Hall.

Explain why change is necessary before implementation.   **2.1.12**

Conger, J. A. (1989). The charismatic leader: Behind the mystique of exceptional leadership. San Francisco: Jossey-Bass.

Duval, S., & Wicklund, R. A. (1972). A theory of objective self-awareness. New York: Academic Press.

Nanus, B. (1992). Visionary leadership. San Francisco: Jossey-Bass.

Sashkin, M., & Burke, W. W. (1990). Understanding and assessing organizational leadership. In Clark, K.. E., & Clark, M. B. (Eds.). *Measures of leadership* (pp. 297–325). West Orange, NJ: Leadership Library of America.

Tichy, N. M., & Devanna, M. A. (1986). The transformational leader. New York: John Wiley & Sons.

2.1.13   Clearly communicate what will and will not change.

Burke, W. W., & Trahant, W. (2000). Business climate shifts: Profiles of change makers. Boston: Butterworth-Heineman.

Goodstein, L. D., & Burke, W. W. (1991, Spring). Creating successful organizational change. *Organizational Dynamics*, 19(4), 5–17.

Holmes, T. H., & Raye, R. H. (1967). The social readjustment scale. *Journal of Psychological Research*, 11, 213–218.

2.1.14   Develop an exit strategy for outsourcing agreements.

Axson, D. A. J. (2003). Best practices in planning and management reporting: From data to decisions. New York: John Wiley & Sons.

Barthélemy, J. (2003). The seven deadly sins of outsourcing. *The Academy of Management Executive*, 17(2), 87–100.

2.1.15   Use benchmarking to improve organizational practice.

Fitz-enz, J. (1993, December). How to make benchmarking work for you. *HR Magazine*, 38(12), 40–47.

Karlof, B., & Ostblom, S. (1993). Benchmarking: A signpost to excellence in quality and productivity. New York: John Wiley & Sons.

2.1.16   Share experience and best practices across business units.

Baumbusch, R. (1997). Internal best practices: Turning knowledge into results. *Strategy & Leadership*, 44–45.

O'Dell, C., & Grayson, C. J. (1998, Spring). If only we knew what we know: Identification and transfer of internal best practices. *California Management Review*, 154–174.

2.1.17   Assess training needs before implementing a training program.

Moore, M. L., & Dutton, P. (1978, July). Training needs analysis: Review and critique. *Academy of Management Review*, 3(3), 532–545.

Porter, M. E. (1985). Competitive advantage. New York: The Free Press.

2.1.18   Strive to eliminate all forms of excess and waste.

Green, M., & Berry, J. F. (1985). The challenge of hidden profits: Reducing bureaucracy and waste. New York: William Morrow and Company, Inc.

Kaplan, R. S., & Norton, D. P. (1996). The balanced scorecard: Translating strategy into action. Boston: Harvard Business School Press.

Maceda, M., Corbett, A., & Altman, V. (2003, May/June). Finding hidden profits. *Journal of Business Strategy*, 24(3), 36–40.

Welch, J. F. (2000). Removing walls. In Krass, P. (Ed.). *The book of management wisdom: Classic writings by legendary managers* (pp. 359–364). New York: John Wiley & Sons.

Witzel, M. (2002, Winter). A short history of efficiency. *Business Strategy Review*, 13(4), 38–47.

Womack, J. P., & Jones, D. T. (1996). Lean thinking: Banish waste and create wealth in your corporation. New York: Simon & Schuster.

Simplify systems and procedures.   **2.2.1**

Jensen, B. (2001). Simplicity: The new competitive advantage in a world of more, better, faster. Cambridge, MA: Perseus Publishing.

Kanin-Lovers, J., & Miller, D. (1994, January/February). Adopting a simple framework. *Journal of Compensation & Benefits*, 9(4), 57–60.

Schonberger, R. J. (1986). World class manufacturing: The lessons of simplicity applied. New York: The Free Press.

Trout, J., & Rivkin, S. (2001). The power of simplicity: A management guide to cutting through the nonsense and doing things right. New York: McGraw-Hill Trade.

Centralize policy and decentralize management.   **2.2.2**

Blanchard, K., Carlos, J. P., & Randolph, A. (1999). The 3 keys to empowerment: Release the power within people for astonishing results. San Francisco: Berrett-Koehler.

Lawler III, E. E., Mohrman, S. A., & Benson, G. (2001). Organizing for high performance organizations: Employee involvement, TQM, reengineering, and knowledge management in the Fortune 1000. San Francisco: Josscy-Bass.

Liebling, B. A. (1981, September). Riding the organizational pendulum . . . Is it time to (de)centralize? *Management Review*, 70(9), 14–20.

Perrow, C. (1977, Spring). The bureaucratic paradox: The efficient organization centralizes in order to decentralize. *Organizational Dynamics*, 5(4), 3–14.

Sloan, Jr., A. P. (2000). Modern ideals of big business. In P. Krass (Ed.). *The book of management wisdom: Classic writings by legendary managers* (pp. 311–319). New York: John Wiley & Sons.

Zábojník, J. (2002). Centralized and decentralized decision making in organizations. *Journal of Labor Economics*, 20(1), 1–22.

Insulate research and development teams from market feedback and internal politics.   **2.2.3**

Christensen, C. M., & Bower, J. L. (1995, March). Customer power, strategic investment, and the failure of leading firms. *Strategic Management Journal*, 17, 197–218.

Kessler, E. H., Bierly III, P. E., & Gopalakrishnan, S. (2001, August). Vasa syndrome: Insights from a 17th-century new-product disaster. *The Academy of Management Executive*, 15(3), 80–91.

2.2.4   **Design jobs that possess high-core job dimensions.**

Judge, T. A., Bono, J. E., & Locke, E. A. (2000, April). Personality and job satisfaction: The mediating role of job characteristics. *Journal of Applied Psychology*, 237–249.

Loher, B. T., Noe, R. A., Moeller, N. L., & Fitzgerald, M. P. (1985, May). A meta-analysis of the relationship of job characteristics to job satisfaction. *Journal of Applied Psychology*, 280–289.

Rentsch, J. R., & Steel, R. P. (1998). Testing the durability of job characteristics as predictors of absenteeism over a six year period. *Personnel Psychology*, 165–190.

2.2.5   **Provide employees with "whole" tasks.**

Hackman, J. R., & Oldham, G. R. (1980). Work redesign. Reading, MA: Addison-Wesley.

2.2.6   **Separate responsibility for task completion from responsibility for task assistance.**

Byham, W. C., & Cox, J. (1988). Zapp! The lightning of empowerment: How to improve productivity, quality, and employee satisfaction. New York: Harmony Books.

Manove, M. (1997, January). Job responsibility, pay, and promotion. *The Economic Journal*, 107(440), 85–103.

2.2.7   **Maintain an up-to-date organizational chart.**

Chandler, Jr., A. D. (1988, March/April). Origins of the organization chart. *Harvard Business Review*, 66(2), 156–157.

Fanning, M. M. (1997, Summer). A circular organization chart promotes a hospital wide focus on teams. *Hospital & Health Services Administration*, 243–254.

Mintzberg, H., & Van der Heyden, L. (1999, September/October). Organigraphs: Drawing how companies really work. *Harvard Business Review*, 87–94.

2.2.8   **Actively support telecommuting or do not use it at all.**

Igbaria, M., & Guimaraes, T. (1999, Summer). Exploring differences in employee turnover intentions and its determinants among telecommuters and non-telecommuters. *Journal of Management Information Systems*, 16(1), 147–164.

Knight, P. J., & Westbrook, J. (1999, March). Comparing employees in traditional job structures vs. telecommuting jobs using Herzberg's hygienes & motivations. *Engineering Management Journal*, 11(1), 15–20.

Kurland, N. B., & Bailey, D. E. (1999, Autumn). Telework: The advantages and challenges of working here, there, anywhere, and anytime. *Organizational Dynamics*, 28(2), 53–67.

2.2.9   **Institute formal, direct lines of communication between executives and employees.**

Argenti, P. A. (1998, Fall/Winter). Strategic employee communications. *Human Resource Management*, 199–206.

Sanchez, P. (1999, August/September). How to craft successful employee communication in the information age. *Communication World*, 9–15.

Spitzer, R., & Swindler, M. (2003, Spring). Using a marketing approach to improve internal communications. *Employment Relations Today*, 69–82.

Set direction about ends, but not means.   2.3.1

Hackman, J. R. (2002). Leading teams: Setting the stage for great performances. Boston: Harvard Business School Press.

Keep teams small.   2.3.2

Curral, L. A., Forrester, R. H., Dawson, J. F., & West, M. A. (2001, June). It's what you do and the way you do it: Team task, team size, and innovation-related group processes. *European Journal of Work and Organizational Psychology*, 10(2), 187–204.

Hackman, J. R. (2002). Leading teams: Setting the stage for great performances. Boston: Harvard Business School Press.

Keep teams together—they only get better with time.   2.3.3

Cohen, S. G., & Bailey, D. E. (1997). What makes teams work: Group effectiveness research from the shop floor to the executive suite. *Journal of Management*, 23, 239–290.

Katz, R. (1982). The effects of group longevity on project communication and performance. *Administrative Science Quarterly*, 27, 81–104.

Katzenbach, J. R., & Smith, D. K. (1993). The wisdom of teams: Creating the high-performance organization. Boston: Harvard University Press.

Ensure that new teams realize early success.   2.3.4

Hackman, J. R. (2002). Leading teams: Setting the stage for great performances. Boston: Harvard Business School Press.

Katz, N., & Koenig, G. (2001, August). Sports teams as a model of workplace teams: Lessons and liabilities. *The Academy of Management Executive*, 15(3), 56–70.

Emphasize fairness.   2.3.5

Colquitt, J. (2000). Justice in teams: How the fairness of the one interacts with the fairness of many. Paper presented at the National Academy of Management, Toronto.

Colquitt, J. A., Noe, R. A., & Jackson, C. L. (2002, Spring). Justice in teams: Antecedents and consequences of procedural justice. *Personnel Psychology*, 55(1), 83–100.

Ensure the contribution of all team members.   2.3.6

Kravitz D. A., & Martin, B. (1986, May). Ringelman rediscovered: The original article. *Journal of Personality and Social Psychology*, 50(5), 936–941.

Miles, J. A., & Greenberg, J. (1993, November). Using punishment threats to attenuate social loafing effects among swimmers. *Organizational Behavior and Human Decision Processes*, 56(2), 246–265.

Nordstrom, R. R., Lorenzi, P. H., & Hall, R. V. (1990). A review of public posting of performance feedback in work settings. *Journal of Organizational Behavior Management*, 11(2), 101–123.

2.3.7   **Create a war room for projects requiring high levels of interaction.**

Teasley, S., Covi, L., Krishnan, M. S., & Olson, J. S. (2000). How does radical collocation help a team succeed? In Proceedings of the CSCW 2000. Philadelphia: Association for Computing Machinery, 339–346.

2.3.8   **Favor group-based rewards over individual-based rewards.**

Balkin, D., & Gomez-Mejia, L. (1984). Determinants of R&D compensation strategies in the high tech industry. *Personnel Psychology*, 37, 635–650.

Johnson, D., & Johnson, R. (1989). Cooperation and competition: Theory and research. Edina, MN: Interaction Book Company.

Mesch, D., Lew, M., Johnson, D., & Johnson, R. (1988). Impact of positive interdependence and academic group contingencies on achievement. *The Journal of Social Psychology*, 128, 345–352.

Milkovich, G., & Newman, J. (1990). Compensation. Homewood, IL: BPI/Irwin.

Milkovich, G., & Wigdor, A. (1991). Pay for performance: Evaluating performance appraisal and merit pay. Washington, DC: National Academy Press.

2.3.9   **Structure common tasks and share rewards to improve group cohesion.**

Deutsch, M. (1949). A theory of cooperation and competition. *Human Relations*, 2, 129–152.

Johnson, D. W., Maruyama, G., Johnson, R. T., Nelson, D., & Skon, L. (1981). Effects of cooperative, competitive and individualistic goal structures on achievement: A meta-analysis. *Psychological Bulletin*, 89, 47–62.

Stanne, M. B., Johnson, D. W., & Johnson, R. T. (1999, January). Does competition enhance or inhibit motor performance: A meta-analysis. *Psychological Bulletin*, 125(1), 133–154.

3.1.1   **Hire internally when qualified candidates are available.**

Collins, J. (2001). Good to great: Why some companies make the leap . . . and others don't. New York: HarperCollins.

Friedman, S. D. (1991). Why hire from within? Causes and consequences of internal promotion systems. *Academy of Management Best Papers Proceedings*, 272–276.

3.1.2   **Implement a coworker referral program.**

Fernandez, R., & Weinberg, N. (1997, December). Sifting and sorting: Personal contacts and hiring in a retail bank. *American Sociological Review*, 62(6), 883–902.

3.1.3   **Provide job candidates with a realistic job preview.**

Phillips, J. M. (1998, December). Effects of realistic job previews on multiple organizational outcomes: A meta-analysis. *The Academy of Management Journal*, 41(6), 673–690.

Wanous, J. P. (1989, Spring). Installing a realistic job preview: Ten tough choices. *Personnel Psychology*, 42(1), 117–133.

Use psychometric tools as guides only. **3.1.4**

Funder, D. C. (1999). Personality judgment: A realistic approach to person perception. San Diego: Academic Press.

Moustafa, K. S., & Miller, T. R. (2003, Spring). Too intelligent for the job? The validity of upper-limit cognitive ability test scores in selection. *SAM Advanced Management Journal*, 68(2), 4–10.

Consider general mental ability in hiring practices. **3.1.5**

LePine, J. A., Colquitt, J. A., & Erez, A. (2000). Adaptability to changing task contexts: Effects of general cognitive ability, conscientiousness, and openness to experience. *Personnel Psychology*, 53, 563–593.

Ree, M. J., Earles, J. A., & Teachout, M. S. (1994). Predicting job performance: Not much more than g. *Journal of Applied Psychology*, 79, 518–524.

Rynes, S. L., Brown, K. G., & Colbert, A. E. (2002). Seven common misconceptions about human resource practices: Research findings versus practitioners beliefs. *The Academy of Management Executive*, 16(3), 92–103.

Use situational interviews. **3.1.6**

Latham, G. P. (1989). The reliability, validity, and practicality of the situational interview. In Ferris, G., & Eder, R. (Eds.). *The employment interview: Theory, research and practice* (pp. 169–182). Newbury Park, CA: Sage Publications.

Latham, G. P., & Sue-Chan, C. (1996). A legally defensible interview for selecting the best. In Barrett, R. S. (Ed.). Fair employment strategies. Westport, CT: Quorum Books.

Latham, G. P., & Sue-Chan, C. (1999, February). A meta-analysis of the situational interview: An enumerative review of reasons for its validity. *Canadian Psychology*, 40(1), 56–67.

Consider high-performance personality traits in hiring practices. **3.1.7**

Goffin, R. D., & Rothstein, M. G. (1996, December). Personality testing and the assessment center: Incremental validity for managerial selection. *Journal of Applied Psychology*, 81(6), 746–756.

Mount, M. K., & Barrick, M. R. (1995, May). The big five personality dimensions: Implication for research and practice in human resource management. In Rowland, K. M., & Ferris, G. (Eds.). Research in personnel and human resources management, 13. Greenwich, CT: JAI Press.

Salgado, J. F. (1997, February). The five-factor model of personality and job performance in the European community. *Journal of Applied Psychology*, 82(1), 30–43.

Inform job applicants of reference checks. **3.1.8**

Knouse, S. B. (1987). An attribution theory approach to the letter of recommendation. *International Journal of Management*, 4(1), 5–13.

Ryan, A. M., & Lasek, M. (1991). Negligent hiring and defamation: Areas of liability related to pre-employment inquiries. *Personnel Psychology*, 44(2), 293–319.

Smart, B. D. (1999). Topgrading: How leading companies win by hiring, coaching and keeping the best people. Upper Saddle River, NJ: Prentice Hall Press.

3.1.9   Focus on cultural fit and value congruence.

Chatman, J. A. (1991). Matching people and organizations: Selection and socialization in public accounting firms. *Administrative Science Quarterly*, 36(3), 459–484.

Meglino, B. M., & Ravlin, E. C. (1998). Individual values in organizations: Concepts, controversies, and research. *Journal of Management*, 24(3), 351–389.

3.2.1   Treat employees as assets of the organization, not costs.

Cascio, W. F. (2003). Managing human resources. Boston: McGraw-Hill Irwin.

Davenport, T. O. (1999). Human capital: What it is and why people invest it. San Francisco: Jossey-Bass.

Drucker, P. (1995). Managing in a time of great change. New York: Truman Talley Books/Dutton.

Fitz-enz, J. (2000). The ROI of human capital. New York: AMACOM.

3.2.2   Hold managers accountable for employee retention.

Mitchell, T. R., Holtom, B. C., & Lee, T. W. (2001). How to keep your best employees: Developing an effective retention policy. *The Academy of Management Executive*, 15(4), 96–108.

Steel, R. P., Griffeth, R., & Hom, P. W. (2002). Practical retention policy for the practical manager. *The Academy of Management Executive*, 16(2), 149–164.

3.2.3   Ensure that employees understand their benefits.

Collison, J. (2002, August). Corporate credibility and an employee communications survey. Society for Human Resource Management/Council of Public Relations Firms.

Emerson, J. (2003, October). The high cost of poor benefits communication. *Human Capital*, 5, 10–14.

Kennan, B. (1999, Summer). Internet technology and employee benefits. *Journal of Pension Planning and Compliance*, 25, 16–40.

Sweeney, W. J. (2002, June). Utilizing benefit communication technology. *Employee Benefits Journal*, 27, 19–22.

3.2.4   Conduct exit interviews when employees resign.

Brotherton, P. (1996). Exit interviews can provide a reality check. *HR Magazine*, 41(8), 45–49.

Giacalone, R. A., & Duhon, D. (1991). Assessing intended employee behavior in exit interviews. *Journal of Psychology*, 125(1), 83–90.

Jurkiewicz, C. L., Knouse, S. B., & Giacalone, R. A. (2002, Spring). Are exit interviews and surveys really worth the time and effort? *Review of Public Personnel Administration*, 22(1), 52–62.

Knouse, S. B., & Beard, J. W. (1996). Willingness to discuss exit interview topics: the impact of attitudes toward supervisor and authority. *Journal of Psychology*, 130(3), 249–261.

Steel, R. P., Griffeth, R. W., & Horn, P. W. (2002, May). Practical retention policy for the practical manager. *The Academy of Management Executive*, 16(2), 149–162.

Honor the past.   **3.2.5**

Deeprose, D. (2003). Smart things to know about culture. San Francisco: Jossey-Bass.

Wilkins, A. L., & Bristow, N. J. (1987, August). For successful organization culture: Honor your past. *The Academy of Management Executive*, 1(3), 221–229.

Use the past as a source for inspiration and instruction.   **3.2.6**

Coffman, C., & Gonzales-Molina, G. (2002). Follow this path: How the world's greatest organizations drive growth by unleashing human potential. New York: Warner Books.

Neuhauser, P. C. (1993). Corporate legends and lore: The power of storytelling as a management tool. New York: McGraw-Hill.

Pindorf, M. K. (1999, Winter). Building a business on virtue: Actual image, or spin. *Business & Economic History*, 28(2), 185–199.

Create environments where employment security is assured.   **3.2.7**

Maslow, A. H., Frager, R., & Fadiman, J. (1987). Motivation and personality (3rd ed.). Boston: Addison-Wesley.

Pfeffer, J., & Veiga, J. F. (1999, May). Putting people first for organizational success. *The Academy of Management Executive*, 13(2), 37–48.

Create an environment that is work/life friendly.   **3.2.8**

Beauvais, L., & Lyness, K. (1999). When work-family benefits are not enough: The influence of work-family culture on benefit utilization, organizational attachment, and work-family conflict. *Journal of Vocational Behavior*, 54(3), 392–415.

Kofodimos, J. (1993). Balancing Act. San Francisco: Jossey-Bass.

Kossek, E., & Ozeki, C. (1999, April). Bridging the work-family policy and productivity gap: A literature review. *Community, Work & Family*, 2(1), 7–30.

Treat employees the same.   **3.2.9**

Bennett-Alexander, D. D., & Hartman, L. P. (2003). Employment law for business, New York: McGraw-Hill.

Steingold, F. S., Delpo, A., & Guerin, L. (2003). The employer's legal handbook (5th ed.). Berkeley, CA: Nolo Press.

3.2.10   Seek ways to minimize stress.

Benson, H. (1975). The relaxation response. New York: Avon Books.

Pretrus, T., & Kleiner, B. H. (2003, June). New developments concerning workplace safety training: Managing stress arising from work. *Management Research News*, 26(6), 68–76.

Whetton, D. A., & Cameron, K. S. (1998). Developing management skills. Reading, MA: Addison-Wesley.

3.2.11   Develop systems that ensure organizational fairness and justice.

Colquitt, J. A., Conlon, D. E., Wesson, M. J., Porter, C. O. L. H., & Yee Ng, K. (2001, June). Justice at the millennium: A meta-analytic review of 25 years of organizational justice research. *Journal of Applied Psychology*, 86(3), 425–445.

Dailey, R. C., & Kirk, D. J. (1992, March). Distributive and procedural justice as antecedents of job satisfaction and intent to turnover. *Human Relations*, 45(3), 305–317.

Dessler, G. (1999, May). How to earn your employees' commitment. *The Academy of Management Executive*, 13(2), 58–67.

3.2.12   Deal with morale problems.

Abbott, J. (2003, May). Does employee satisfaction matter? A study to determine whether low employee morale affects customer satisfaction and profits in the business-to-business sector. *Journal of Communication Management*, 7, 333–339.

Lawler III, E. E., & Finegold, D. (2000, September). Individualizing the organization: Past, present, and future. *Organizational Dynamics*, 29, 1–14.

Lord, R., Klimoski, R. J., & Kanfer, R. (Eds.) (2002). Emotions in the workplace: Understanding the structure and role of emotions in organizational behavior. San Francisco: Jossey-Bass.

Rubenstein, B. (2000, July). Morale problems hit the Lockheed Martin legal department. *Corporate Legal Times*, 10, 1–4.

3.2.13   Do not avoid or suppress conflict—manage it openly.

De Dreu, C. K. W., Weingart, L. R., & Kwon, S. (2000). Influence of social motivations on integrative negotiation: A meta-analytic review and test of two theories. *Journal of Personality and Social Psychology*, 78, 889–905.

Deutsch, M. (1973). The resolution of conflict. New Haven, CT: Yale University Press.

Tjosvold, D. (1998, July). The cooperative and competitive goal approach to conflict: Accomplishments and challenges. *Applied Psychology: An International Review*, 47(3), 285–313.

Build trust in organizations.   **3.2.14**

Butler, Jr., J. K. (1991). Toward understanding and measuring the conditions of trust: Evolution of a conditions of trust inventory. *Journal of Management*, 17(3), 643–663.

Jones, G. R., & George, J. M. (1998). The experience and evolution of trust: Implications for cooperation and teamwork. *Academy of Management Review*, 23(3), 531–546.

Mayer, R. C., & Davis, J. H. (1995). An integrative model of organizational trust. *Academy of Management Review*, 20(3), 709–734.

Oliver, N. (1990). Rewards, investments, alternatives, and organizational commitment: Empirical evidence and theoretical development. *Journal of Occupational Psychology*, 63, 19–31.

Randall, D. M. (1990). The consequences of organizational commitment: Methodological investigation. *Journal of Organizational Behavior*, 11, 361–378.

Taylor, R. G. (1990, Fall). Trust and influence in the workplace. *Organization Development Journal*, 8, 33–36.

Consider layoffs as a cost-reduction method of last resort.   **3.2.15**

Cascio, W. F. (2002). Strategies for responsible restructuring. *The Academy of Management Executive*, 16(3), 80–91.

Favor market-based compensation for base salaries.   **3.2.16**

Deci, E. L., Koestner, R., & Ryan, R. M. (1999). A meta-analytic review of experiments examining the effects of extrinsic rewards on intrinsic motivation. *Psychological Bulletin*, 125, 627–668.

Kohn, A. (1993, September/October). Why incentive plans cannot work. *Harvard Business Review*, 71, 54–63.

Wiersma, U. J. (1992). The effects of extrinsic rewards in intrinsic motivation: A meta-analysis. *Journal of Occupational and Organizational Psychology*, 65, 101–114.

Use performance appraisals for employee development only.   **3.3.1**

Dalessio, A. T. (1998). Using multisource feedback for employee development and personnel decisions. In Smither, J. W. (Ed.). *Performance appraisal: State of the art in practice* (pp. 278–330). San Francisco: Jossey Bass.

Murphy, K. R., & Cleveland, J. N. (1995). Understanding performance appraisal: Social, organizational, and goal-based perspectives. Thousand Oaks, CA: Sage Publications.

Meet with employees on a regular basis to discuss performance.   **3.3.2**

Edwards, J. E., Scott, J. C., & Raju, N. S. (2003). The human resources program-evaluation handbook. Thousand Oaks, CA: Sage Publications.

Pipe, P., & Mager, R. F. (1999). Analyzing performance problems. New York: The Center For Effective Performance.

Smither, J. W. (Ed.). (1998). Performance appraisal: State of the art in practice. San Francisco: Jossey-Bass.

3.3.3   Cultivate creativity, risk taking, and contrarian thinking.

Amabile, T. M. (1993). Motivational synergy: Toward new conceptualizations of intrinsic and extrinsic motivation in the workplace. *Human Resource Management Review*, 3, 185–201.

Jassawalla, A. R., & Sashittal, H. C. (2002, August). Cultures that support product innovation processes. *The Academy of Management Executive*, 16(3), 42–54.

Kanter, R. M. (1983). The change masters. New York: Simon & Schuster.

3.3.4   Implement a volunteer-only mentor program.

Fagenson, E. A. (1992). Mentoring: Who needs it? A comparison of protégé's and nonprotégé's needs for power, achievement, affiliation, and autonomy. *Journal of Vocational Behavior*, 41(1), 48–60.

Jossi, F. (1997, August). Mentoring in changing times. *Training*, 34(8) 50–54.

Kram, K. E. (1985). Mentoring at work: Developmental relationships in organizational life. Glenview, IL: Scott Foresman.

3.3.5   Implement career development programs.

Buckingham, M., & Clifton, D. O. (2001). Now discover your strengths. New York: The Free Press.

Zander, R. S., & Zander, B. (2000). The art of possibility: Transforming professional and personal life. Boston: Harvard Business School Press.

3.3.6   Use multisource feedback to evaluate performance.

London, M. (2003). Job feedback: Giving, seeking, and using feedback for performance improvement (2nd ed.). Mahwah, NJ: Lawrence Erlbaum Associates.

London, M., & Smither, J. W. (1995, Winter). Can multisource feedback change perceptions of goal accomplishment, self-evaluations, and performance related outcomes? Theory-based applications and directions for research. *Personnel Psychology*, 48(4), 803–839.

Mount, M. K., Judge, T. A., Scullen, S. E., Sytsma, M. R., & Hezlett, S. A. (1998, Autumn). Trait, rater and level effects in 360-degree performance ratings. *Personnel Psychology*, 51(3), 557–576.

3.3.7   Avoid similar-to-me bias.

Eidson, Jr., C. E., & Gurman, E. B. (1998, Fall). Similarity bias and ratings of applicants: Fact or artifact? *Journal of Business and Psychology*, 13(1), 81–84.

Pulakos, E. D., & Wexley, K. N. (1983). The relationship among perceptual similarity, sex, and performance rating in manager-subordinated dyads. *The Academy of Management Journal*, 26(1), 129–139.

Schaubroeck, J., & Lam, S. S. K. (2002). How similarity to peers and supervisor influences organizational advancement in different cultures. *The Academy of Management Journal*, 45(6), 1120–1136.

Turban, D. B., & Jones, A. P. (1988). Supervisor-subordinate similarity: Types, effects, and mechanisms. *Journal of Applied Psychology*, 73(2) 228–234.

Favor developing strengths over correcting weaknesses.   **3.3.8**

Buckingham, M., & Clifton, D. O. (2001). Now discover your strengths. New York: The Free Press.

LeDoux, J. (2002). Synaptic self: How our brains become who we are. New York: Viking Press.

Create a culture that is receptive to continuous change.   **3.3.9**

Kriegel, R., & Brandt, D. (1996). Sacred cows make the best burgers: Developing change-ready people and organizations. New York: Warner Books.

Schweiger, D. M., Sandberg, W. R., & Rechner, P. L. (1989, December). Experiential effects of dialectical inquiry, devil's advocacy, and consensus approaches to strategic decision making. *The Academy of Management Journal*, 32(4), 745–772.

Tjosvold, D. (1985, Fall/Winter). Implications of controversy research for management. *Journal of Management*, 11(3), 21–37.

Empower employees with authority and accountability.   **3.3.10**

Gunn, B. (2003, January). Delegating decisions. *Strategic Finance*, 84(7), 11–12.

Lewis, B. J. (2000, March/April). Management by delegation. *Journal of Management in Engineering*, 16(2), 21.

Messmer, M. (2000, March). Delegating for results. *Strategic Finance*, 81(9), 8–9.

Portney, S. E. (2002, March/April). The delegation dilemma: When do you let it go? *Information Management Journal*, 36(2), 60–64.

Emphasize "learning from experience" to develop leadership.   **3.3.11**

Boyatzis, R. (1982). The competent manager: A model for effective performance. New York: John Wiley & Sons.

Lombardo, M., & Eichinger, R. (2002). The leadership machine. Minneapolis: Lominger Limited.

Lombardo, M., & Eichinger, R. (2003). The LEADERSHIP ARCHITECT® Norms and Validity Report. Minneapolis: Lominger Limited.

McCall, M., & Lombardo, M. (1983, February). What makes a top executive? *Psychology Today*, 17(2), 26–31.

McCall, M., Lombardo, M., & Morrison, A. (1988). The lessons of experience. Lexington, MA: Lexington Books.

McCauley, C. D., Ruderman, M. N., Ohlott, P. J., & Morrow, J. E. (1994, August). Assessing the developmental components of managerial jobs. *Journal of Applied Psychology*, 79(4), 544–560.

3.4.1   Put employees first. Shareholder value will follow.

Becker, B., & Gerhart, B. (1996). The impact of human resource management on organizational performance: Progress and prospects. *The Academy of Management Journal*, 39(4), 779–801.

Bridges, S., Marcum, W., & Harrison, J. K. (2003, Spring). The relation between employee perceptions of stakeholder balance and corporate financial performance. *SAM Advanced Management Journal*, 68(2), 50–55.

Pfeffer, J., & Veiga, J. F. (1999). Putting people first for organizational success. *The Academy of Management Executive*, 13(2), 37–49.

Tsui, A. S., Pearce, J. L., Porter, L. W., & Tripoli, A. M. (1997). Alternative approaches to the employee-organization relationship: Does investment in employees pay off? *The Academy of Management Journal*, 40, 1089–1121.

3.4.2   Avoid internal competition. Emphasize external competition.

Deming, W. E. (2000). The new economics for industry, government, Education (2nd ed.). Cambridge, MA: MIT Press.

Pfeffer, J., & Sutton, R. (2002). The knowing-doing gap: How smart companies turn knowledge into action. Boston: Harvard Business School Press.

3.4.3   Cultivate a stakeholder culture.

Geer, C. T. (1997). Turning employees into stakeholders. *Forbes*, 160(12), 154–156.

Jones, D. (1997, Summer). Employees as stakeholders. *Business Strategy Review*, 8(2), 21–4.

Pfeffer, J. (2003, March). Do options really motivate? *Business 2.0*, (4), 66.

Pierce, J. L., Kostova, T., & Dirks, K. T. (2001, April). Toward a theory of psychological ownership in organizations. *Academy of Management Review*, 26(2), 298–310.

Welch, J. (2002). Stock-option cultures: Employee ownership in a high-growth software company. *Academy of Management Proceedings*, H1–H6.

3.4.4   Minimize status distinctions.

Pfeffer, J., & Veiga, J. F. (1999, May). Putting people first for organizational success. *The Academy of Management Executive*, 13(2), 37–48.

Tjosvold, D., Motohiro, M., & Belsheim, J. A. (1999). Complaint handling on the shop floor: Cooperative relationships and open-minded strategies. *International Journal of Conflict Management*, 10(1), 45–68.

3.4.5   Maintain a positive emotional climate.

Ashkanasy, N. M., & Daus, C. S. (2002). Emotion in the workplace: The new challenge for managers. *The Academy of Management Executive*, 16(1), 76–86.

Barsade, S. G. (2002). The ripple effect: Emotional contagion and its influence on group behavior. *Administrative Science Quarterly*, 47(4), 644–675.

Goleman, D. (1995). Emotional intelligence. New York: Bantam Books.

Özçelik, H., Langton, N., & Aldrich, H. (2001). Does intention to create a positive emotional climate matter? A look at revenue, strategic and outcome growth. *Academy of Management Proceedings*, G1–G6.

Tsai, W. (2001). Determinants and consequences of employee displayed positive emotions. *Journal of Management*, 27(4), 497–512.

Share the rewards of success with all employees. **3.4.6**

Bloom, M. (1999, February). The performance effects of pay dispersion on individuals and organizations. *The Academy of Management Journal*, 42(1), 25–40.

Graham-Moore, B., & Ross, T. L. (1990). Gainsharing: Plan for improving performance. Washington, DC: Bureau of National Affairs.

Hanlon, S. C., Meyer, D. C., & Taylor, R. R. (1994). Consequences of gainsharing: A field experiment revisited. *Group and Organizational Management*, 19(1), 87–111.

Pfeffer, J. (1996, Winter). Seven practices of successful organizations. *California Management Review*, 40(2), 96–124.

Label different business and management eras. **3.4.7**

Collins, J. C., & Porras, J. I. (2002). Built to last: Successful habits of visionary companies. New York: HarperCollins.

Trice, H. M., & Beyer, J. M. (1993). The culture of work organizations. Englewood Cliffs, NJ: Prentice Hall.

Wilkins, A. L., & Bristow, N. J. (1987, August). For successful organization culture, honor your past. *The Academy of Management Executive*, 1(3), 221–228.

Engage employees in organization-sponsored community outreach. **3.4.8**

Greening, D. W., & Turban, D. B. (2000). Corporate social performance as a competitive advantage in attracting a quality workforce. *Business and Society*, 39, 254–280.

Melohn, T. (1996). The new partnership: Profit by bringing out the best in your people, customers, and yourself. New York: John Wiley & Sons.

Actively promote team spirit in groups. **3.4.9**

Campion, M. A., Papper, E. M., & Medsker, G. J. (1996, Summer). Relations between work team characteristics and effectiveness: A replication and extension. *Personnel Psychology*, 49(2), 429–452.

Colquitt, J. A., Noe, R. A., & Jackson, C. L. (2002). Justice in teams: Antecedents and consequences of procedural justice climate. *Personnel Psychology*, 55, 83–100.

Wageman, R. (1997, Summer). Critical success factors for creating superb self-managing teams. *Organizational Dynamics*, 26(1), 49–61.

Werner, J. M. (1995). Managing a multicultural team. *Business & Economic Review*, 41(2), 15–18.

Werner, J. M. (1997). Measuring the performance of student case teams: A team audit instrument. *Academy of Management Proceedings*, 215–219.

3.4.10   **Emphasize listening in discussions and meetings.**

Baskin, O. W., & Aronoff, C. E. (1980). Interpersonal communication in organizations. Santa Monica, CA: Goodyear.

Burley-Allen, M. (1995). Listening the forgotten skill: A self-teaching guide. New York: John Wiley & Sons.

Fusaro, R. (2000, September/October). Peer to peer. *Harvard Business Review*, 78(5), 32.

3.4.11   **De-emphasize the hierarchy of the organizational chart.**

George, Jr., C. S. (1972). The history of management thought. Upper Saddle River, NJ: Prentice Hall.

Tsaklanganos, A. A. (1973/1984). The organization chart: A managerial myth. *SAM Advanced Management Journal*, 38(2), 53–57.

Wren, D. A. (1994). The evolution of management thought (4th ed.). New York: John Wiley & Sons.

3.4.12   **Focus on fixing problems, not punishing people.**

Martin, G. L., & Pear, J. (2002). Behavior modification: What it is and how to do it. Saddle River, NJ: Prentice Hall.

Miltenberger, R. G. (2000). Behavior modification: Principles and procedures. Cincinnati: Wadsworth Publishing.

3.4.13   **Share key financial information with employees.**

Barton, T. L., Shenkir, W. G., & Tyson, T. N. (1990). Open-book management: Creating an ownership culture. New York: Financial Executives Research Foundation.

Case, J. (1999). The open-book experience: Lessons from over 100 companies who successfully transformed themselves. New York: Perseus Publishing.

READINGS

Michael Beer and Nitin Nohria
Breaking the Code of Change
Harvard Business School Press, 2000

Warren Bennis
On Becoming a Leader: The Leadership Classic—Updated and Expanded
Perseus Publishing, 2003

Marcus Buckingham and Donald Clifton
Now, Discover Your Strengths
The Free Press, 2001

Marcus Buckingham and Curt Coffman
First, Break All the Rules: What the World's Greatest Managers Do Differently
Simon & Schuster, 1999

Warner Burke
Organization Change: Theory and Practice
Sage Publications, 2002

Ram Charan
Boards At Work: How Corporate Boards Create Competitive Advantage
Jossey-Bass, 1998

Clayton Christensen and Michael Raynor
The Innovator's Solution: Creating and Sustaining Successful Growth
Harvard Business School Press, 2003

Jim Collins
Good to Great: Why Some Companies Make the Leap . . . And Others Don't
HarperCollins, 2001

Jim Collins and Jerry Porras
Built to Last: Successful Habits of Visionary Companies
HarperCollins, 1994

Stuart Crainer
The 75 Greatest Management Decisions Ever Made . . . And 21 of the Worst
AMACON, 1999

W. Edwards Deming
Out of the Crisis
Massachusetts Institute of Technology, 1986

William Dimma
Excellence in the Boardroom: Best Practices in Corporate Directorship
John Wiley & Sons, 2002

Peter Drucker
The Essential Drucker
HarperBusiness, 2003

Peter Drucker
Management Challenges for the 21st Century
HarperBusiness, 2001

Sydney Finkelstein
Why Smart Executives Fail, And What You Can Learn from Their Mistakes
Portfolio, 2003

Jeffrey Garten
The Mind of the CEO
Basic Books, 2001

Bill George
Authentic Leadership: Rediscovering the Secrets to Creating Lasting Value
Jossey-Bass, 2003

Robert Greene
48 Laws of Power
Penguin, 2000

Richard Hackman
Leading Teams: Setting the Stage for Great Performances
Harvard Business School Press, 2002

Gary Hamel and C. K. Prahalad
Competing for the Future
Harvard Business School Press, 1994

Charles Handy
Twenty-One Ideas for Managers
Jossey-Bass, 2000

Phil Harkins
Powerful Conversations
McGraw-Hill, 1999

William Joyce and Nitin Nohria
What Really Works: The 4+2 Formula for Sustained Business Success
HarperBusiness, 2003

Rosabeth Moss Kanter
The Change Masters: Innovation for Productivity in the American Corporation
Simon & Schuster, 1983

Robert Kaplan
The Balance Scorecard: Translating Strategy Into Action
Harvard Business School Press, 2000

John Kotter
Leading Change
Harvard Business School Press, 1996

Edwin Locke and Gary Latham
Goal Setting: A Motivational Technique That Works!
Prentice Hall, 1984

Morgan McCall, Jr., Michael Lombardo, and Ann Morrison
The Lessons of Experience: How Successful Executives Develop on the Job
Lexington Books, 1988

Henry Mintzberg, Bruce Ahlstrand, and Joseph Lampel
Strategy Safari: A Guided Tour Through the Wilds of Strategic Management
Simon & Schuster, 1998

Paul Niven
Balanced Scorecard Step-by-Step: Maximizing Performance and Maintaining Results
John Wiley & Sons, 2002

Jeffrey Pfeffer and Robert Sutton
The Knowing-Doing Gap: How Smart Companies Turn Knowledge into Action
Harvard Business School Press, 2000

Michael Porter
Competitive Strategy: Techniques For Analyzing Industries And Competitors
The Free Press, 1998

Edgar Schein
Organizational Culture & Leadership
Jossey-Bass, 1985

Dave Ulrich, Jack Zenger, and Norm Smallwood
Results-Based Leadership
Harvard Business School Press, 1999

INDEX

ABOUT AMSI

The Applied Management Sciences Institute (AMSI) is a private research firm located in Houston, Texas. AMSI Partners and Research Fellows are leading experts from academia and industry. They represent a tremendous depth of scholarly, consulting, and advisory experience, with collective authorship of over 500 books, thousands of articles in the areas of business and management, and extensive experience consulting with organizations of all types and sizes.

AMSI conducts research on how individuals and organizations can optimize their performance. The results of this research are translated into clear, actionable guidelines and published through AMSI Press and AMSI's other publishing partners.

If you have comments or suggestions regarding this book, or would like to propose new guidelines or revisions to existing guidelines, please contact us at research@ams-institute.com. If you would like to learn more about AMSI, please visit us online at www.ams-institute.com.